The

Amazing Laws of
Cosmic Mind Power

Other Books by Joseph Murphy:

THE POWER OF YOUR SUBCONSCIOUS MIND
THE MIRACLE OF MIND DYNAMICS

The

Amazing Laws of Cosmic Mind Power

Joseph Murphy

D.R.S., D.D., Ph.D., LL.D.
Fellow of the Andhra Research,
University of India

PARKER PUBLISHING COMPANY, INC., West Nyack, N.Y.

LIBRARY OF CONGRESS
CATALOG CARD NUMBER: 65-24693

20   19   18   17   PBK

10   9   8   7   RWD CLASSICS PBK

ISBN 0-13-023888-0

PRINTED IN THE UNITED STATES OF AMERICA

How the
Amazing Laws
of cosmic mind power
can change your life

This book can work magic in your life.

Since magic is the production of effects by unknown forces, magic is then a relative term. However, if the processes are known to you, the function is not a work of magic to you. Unless you understand the operation of the radio, television, motion pictures, or phonograph, these could be considered magical devices and actually would have been called magical two hundred years ago. Of course, you would not call them so now, because you know how they operate.

All fundamental forces are, by their nature, unknown. Furthermore, all things are the products of mind, yet we similarly don't know what mind is. We cannot analyze it under a microscope, nor can we see it, but we can find out, nevertheless, how it works; then we discover a hidden power that lifts us up and sets us on the high road to happiness, freedom, and peace of mind.

How You Use Your Magic Power Every Day

We don't know what electricity is, for instance; we only know some of the things it does. This force is still unknown to us. So, you see, all of us actually practice magic all day long. We haven't the slightest idea, for example, of how we move or can lift a finger just by the expressed will of the mind. It is said that the lifting of a finger disturbs the most distant star. So you see that we all are familiar enough with magic, even though it does not go by that name in our common speech. It is only the unaccustomed thing we do not understand that we call magic.

You have a mind and you will learn how to use it more effectively in the pages of this book, and, as a result, wonders will happen in your life.

How This Book Can Change Your Life

This book gives you the key to rebuilding your entire life. It is written for *you*. In the fifteen chapters of this book, there are set forth in simple, practical, down-to-earth language, techniques and processes for using the magical powers of the Universal Mind within you to bring forth health, happiness, and prosperity, plus a feeling of complete inner satisfaction and fulfillment.

In these fifteen carefully written chapters you will read how a man used the magical power of his mind and so could not be hanged, and how another healed himself of both dropsy and glaucoma. Read the fascinating story of a man who used his subconscious mind to become a millionaire.

As you read these captivating and enthralling pages, you will see exactly how these people accomplished startling things through the magical powers within them. This book shows you how to change yourself from *within*. The Magic Power is *within you*. The informative pages show you how to find it and how to use it.

Why None of Your Problems Need to Go Unsolved

There is an answer to every problem. I definitely believe you will find *your* answer in the pages of this book. Here you will learn the methods used by a man to increase his business 300% in a short period of time. You want to live life gloriously. *You can* Read how a young girl gets wonderful slogans for her business which pay her fabulous dividends, and how a novelist gets marvelous ideas through the magic of Mind Power.

Universal Mind Power is the greatest power in the world. Whatever you desire, this Power can fulfill that desire for you, and the Power is your mind, which is one with Universal Mind.

This book shows you *how* to think and *what* to think and how to direct your *mind* so that miracles will also happen in your life. You will find priceless knowledge in these pages which makes it possible for you to banish fear, worry, and jealousy forever—all of which are deadly mental poisons.

Read the fascinating success story of a young man who became president of his organization, and of how a woman's faith in the magical healing power within her healed a malignancy

As you read, and apply the magical power of your mind as outlined herein, you are going on a great and wonderful adventure in mental and spiritual unfoldment. This journey will pay you fabulous dividends in health, wealth, love, and expression. It will prove very exciting, and thereafter you can look forward to the future with joy and enthusiasm. Continue in your marvelous journey through this book until the day breaks and all the shadows flee away

Contents

Law 2 (Cont.)

How His Faith Triumphed
She Changed Her Faith
His Faith Made Him Whole
Faith Is Your Mind
Her Faith in Infinite Intelligence
SERVE YOURSELF WITH FAITH-POWER

Law 3

Healed of Spirit-Voices
She Wasn't Expected to Live
The Natural-Born Healer
Degrees of Faith
A Case of Palsy
He Healed His Withered Hand
How the Hopeless Case Was Healed
Blind Faith and True Faith
How to Give a Spiritual Treatment
VERY PROFITABLE POINTERS
How You Can Face the Word "Incurable" in
Your Own Life
Healing of Dropsy
Steps in Healing
Spiritual Blindness
Vision Is Spiritual, Eternal, and Indestructible
Special Prayer for Eyes and Ears
STEP THIS WAY FOR A HEALING

Law 4

A New Concept of God Works Wonders
The Cause Is Mental

Law 4 (Cont.)

Law 5

The Mysterious Law of Inner Guidance ....

Law 6

The Mighty Law of Courage 87

How Prayer Freed Her from Panic
Her Prayer Cast Out Her Fear
A Garden Gave Him Courage
He Cast Out His Unknown Fears
She Ceased Blocking the Answer
Wise Thoughts
Choose Confidence, Triumph, and Victory
How He Overcame the Feeling of Frustration
Five Positions in Five Months
How to Realize Your Desire
Take a Personal Inventory
Understanding Banishes Needless Suffering
You Create Your Own Heaven
Retribution and Reward
The Secret Place
   IMPORTANT POINTERS

Law 7

The Wonderful Law of Security 103

How to Get the Feeling of Security
He Stopped Praying Against Himself
The End of My Rope
Security Cannot Be Legislated
Pray and Protect Your Investments
Prayer Controlled His Ups and Downs
How She Healed Her Sense of Loss
Building a Glorious Future
   A HEALTHY REVIEW

Law 8

The Magical Law of Mental Nutrition 117

You Are What You Mentally Eat

Law 8 (Cont.)

The Importance of Diet
The Bread of Love and Peace
Your Mental and Spiritual Diet
His Head Knowledge Became Heart Knowledge
His Mental Imagery Healed Him
The Thankful Heart
HIGHLIGHTS TO RECALL

Law 9

Love Is Always Outgoing
How Much Do You Want to Be a New Person?
Why the Actor Failed Three Times
His Prayer of Triumph
Love of God and What It Means
Love and Fear Cannot Dwell Together
Love Conquers Jealousy
The Lord Giveth the Increase
How She Passed Her Examination
Fear Thoughts Can't Hurt You
Become a Spiritual Giant
Lost in the Jungle
Don't Fight Fear
The Enemy in Her Own Mind
Love's Healing Balm
BASIC POINTS TO REMEMBER

Law 10

Becoming Emotionally Mature
Getting the Right Concept of Yourself

Law 10 (Cont.)

Law 11

The Thrilling Law of Marital Harmony 155

Law 12
The Glorious Law of Peace of Mind ....

He Worried About What Had Not Happened
She Healed Her Anxiety Neurosis
Worry Can Cause Diabetes
His Worry Was Not Caused by His Problem
How She Got Off the Merry-Go-Round
You Don't Want It
How Worry Affects All Glands
    and Organs of Our Body
He Raised His Sights
You Can Overcome Worry
Steps in Prayer for Overcoming Worry
    POWER POINTERS

Law 13
The Replenishing Law of Automatic Prosperity ...

How a Broker Prospered
His Subconscious Paid His Mortgage
The Magic of Increase
"Thank You" Opens the Way to Prosperity
She Decreed Prosperity
Life Is Addition
He Began to Sell Again
His Subconscious Made Him a Millionaire
Prayer for Prosperity
    SOME PROFITABLE POINTERS

Law 14
The Penultimate Law of Creation ....

How He Became President
Her Creative Imagination Healed Her

Law 14 (Cont.)

Law 15

The
Astounding Law
of contact with
the cosmic mind

"And all things, whatsoever ye shall ask in prayer, believing, ye shall receive." (Matthew 21:22)

Prayer is always the solution, for God is *". . . a very present help in time of trouble."* (Psalm 46:1) You are instructed to "pray, believing," and you will receive. If this is so—and daily proofs surround us—then prayer is the greatest force in all the world.

No matter what the problem might be, no matter how great the difficulty or how complicated the matter seems to be, prayer can solve it and bring about a happy and joyous solution. After having prayed, you take whatever practical steps seem indicated, because your prayer will guide and direct your footsteps.

Prayer is contacting, communicating, and aligning your thought with the Infinite Intelligence which responds to the nature of your thought and belief. Prayer will bring forth whatever you want and need in your life, if you conform to the laws of your mind purposefully, sincerely, and righteously. Prayer constantly is bringing about the seemingly impossible and healing the so-called incurable. In the history of man, there is no conceivable problem that at some time has not been solved by prayer.

People of all ages, all countries, and all religions have believed in the miraculous power of prayer. "*God is no respecter of persons*" (Acts 10:34) and He is available to all men, regardless of their race, creed, or color. Those who have received marvelous answers to their prayers have either consciously or unconsciously given recognition, honor, and devotion to a responsive Infinite Intelligence which indwells man.

Remember that God is omnipotent, omniscient, and omnipresent, and is untrammeled by time, space, matter, or the vagaries of mankind. It is easy to see, therefore, that there can be no limit to the power of prayer, because "*. . . with God all things are possible.*" (Matthew 19:26)

The Miracle of Prayer

F. L. Rawson, noted engineer and one of England's greatest

scientists, who is the author of *Life Understood*,[1] narrates an account of a British regiment under the command of Colonel Whittlesey that served in World War II for more than five years *without losing a man*. This unparalleled record was made possible by means of the active cooperation of the officers and men, all of whom memorized and repeated regularly the words of the 91st Psalm, which has been called the "Psalm of Protection."

The Ralston Publishing Company of Cleveland, Ohio, prints for distribution wallet-size cards with the above story on one side, under the caption "Protection for Soldiers and Sailors," and the 91st Psalm is on the reverse side.

By constant reiteration and repetition of the truths contained in Psalm 91, the men in Colonel Whittlesey's regiment acquired the feeling of being watched over by an Overshadowing Presence. By repetition, faith, and expectancy, these truths sank down into their subconscious mind, bringing about an inner conviction of Divine protection at all times. This is one of the miracles of prayer.

He Could Not Be Hanged

Some years ago, I read in an article by the late Emma Curtiss Hopkins, author of *Résumé*,[2] of a wonderful event which is recorded in the archives of a state penal institution. This is the essence of the article: Over sixty years ago, a man was sentenced to be hanged. In the interim between his sentence and its time of fulfillment, he sought the love of God and claimed that God would forgive him and free him. The man had committed

---

[1] Published by Wm. Clowes & Sons, Limited, London, England.
[2] Published by Sun Printing Company, Pittsfield, Massachusetts.

the murder for which he had been sentenced, but he had heard or read that God was "the bad man's deliverer." To the great confusion and perplexity of officers of the law, when the man was led to the gallows, the platform, which ordinarily would tip at the slightest weight, became firm the moment the condemned man stepped upon it. They tried again and again to no avail, until finally the prisoner was granted his freedom.

The love of God indeed passes all understanding, and it does illumine the path we tread. The wonders and blessings of God know no ending.

God does not condemn or judge any man. The Bible says: *"Thou art of purer eyes than to behold evil, and canst not look on iniquity . . ."* (Habakkuk 1:13) You pass judgment on yourself by the concepts and beliefs which you entertain. You are always choosing thoughts, thereby passing judgment on yourself. God sees you as perfect. The Perfect One cannot see imperfection. When you rise in consciousness to the point where you forgive yourself and cleanse your mind and heart, the past is forgotten and remembered no more.

Reaping what you have sown turns out to be inexorable only so long as you do not pray or meditate on the truths of God. No matter how awful the crime or heinous the offense, it can be expunged from the mind together with all the punishment that would ordinarily follow. Mere affirmations and perfunctory prayer will not change matters, however. A deep hunger and thirst for God's love and peace, plus an intense desire to reform, are essential in order to wipe out the punishment that must otherwise follow negative and destructive thinking.

I have known murderers in England to be completely transformed by their inner realization of God's love. They were completely "reborn," and they were so changed that it would be impossible for them to repeat the mistakes of the past.

Prayer Can Change Your Life

About twenty years ago, in England, I talked with a man who confessed to me that he had killed a man. He had an intense desire to transform himself and to be reborn mentally and spiritually. I wrote a special prayer for him with instructions on how to apply it at least three times daily, or oftener if he wished. Following is the prayer given to him: For fifteen or twenty minutes, several times daily, he was quietly, silently, and lovingly to claim and feel that God's love, peace, beauty, glory, and joy were flowing through his mind and heart, purifying, cleansing, healing, and restoring his soul. As he did this regularly, these qualities and attributes of God gradually were resurrected within him.

The sequel to his sincere prayer was most interesting and fascinating. After a few months, he told me that one night his whole mind and body, as well as the room he was in, became a blaze of light. Like Paul, he actually was blinded for a while by the light. He said to me that all he could remember was that he knew the whole world was within him and that he felt the ecstasy and rapture of God's love. His feeling was indescribable. It was the moment which lasts forever. Truly, he was a changed man; he experienced and expressed Divine love in his mind and heart. I learned that eventually he began to teach others how to live, and I am sure that he is still doing it somewhere.

You Can Become What You Long to Be

Recently a man came to me for counseling who was unable to hold a job. He drank excessively, was indolent and undependable, and had little determination or vitality. He said that he was interested only in one thing, and that was going to *heaven* when he died.

I explained to him that heaven is the mind at peace and that there is no such thing as physical death,[3] that the only real death is a psychological process wherein you "die" to ignorance, fear, superstition, and sloth, and you resurrect faith, zeal, enthusiasm, confidence, and true expression in life.

He began to pray that Infinite Intelligence would guide and direct him to true expression and that he would prosper spiritually, mentally, and financially. Gradually, he began to develop new interest and excitement in life and to apply himself vigorously to his work, and soon he not only held his job but was promoted to a more responsible position. His new mental attitude changed everything in his life, and he said to me, "I am living in heaven now," by which he meant that he was experiencing health, harmony, and true expression.

How Infinite Intelligence Answered His Prayer

Many years ago I lectured in Auckland, New Zealand, at the Temple of Higher Thought. A man spoke to me at the end of one of my lectures, saying, "I desire desperately to go to New York City to visit my daughter, but I have no money."

I replied to him, "Did you hear the lecture?"

He answered, "Yes, but—"

I suggested that he ignore the doubts in his mind and affirm definitely and positively as follows: "Infinite Intelligence opens up the way for me to visit my daughter in New York City in Divine order." He affirmed this simple prayer several times

[3] See *"Miracle of Mind Dynamics,"* by Joseph Murphy, Page 63 "Every End Is a Beginning," published by Prentice-Hall, Inc., New Jersey, 1964.

daily, and at night he would imagine and feel that he was embracing his daughter and hearing her saying, "Daddy, I am so delighted you're here."

He phoned me at the hotel before I left Auckland and said, "A miracle has happened. A former partner, who had cheated me out of a thousand pounds, relented prior to his death and stipulated that I was to receive this amount at once. In a matter of months, I will be on my way to America."

Infinite Intelligence is all-wise, and It will always respond and react according to the nature of your request. Its ways are past finding out.

Prayer Overcomes Racial Prejudice

A young soldier attached to my battalion in the army said to me, "You know, before the war I tried to get into a certain medical college for several years; they had a quota and I was always turned down because of my race and religion; yet my marks were way above the average."

This young man believed definitely that he was a victim of racial prejudice. I explained to him that Infinite Intelligence is no respecter of persons and It answers all men according to their belief. I discoursed at length with him on the relationship of the conscious and subconscious mind.[4]

He began to understand that his subconscious mind had the answer, that it knew all and had the "know-how" of accomplishment. Accordingly, apropos of the above conversation, the following experiment was suggested to him: At night as he was about to fall asleep, he would imagine that he saw a medical diploma inscribed with his name stating he was a physician and

---

[4] See "*The Power of Your Subconscious Mind*," by Joseph Murphy, Prentice-Hall, Inc., New Jersey, 1963.

surgeon. He felt this diploma with his imaginary hand and felt the joy of it all. He made his mental picture real and natural by focusing his attention on one thing—the diploma—the finished thing; then he contemplated the reality of it. He went to sleep feeling the imaginary diploma in his hand.

The sequel to this soldier's prayer is very interesting. He said to me one morning, "I have a feeling that something is going to happen and that I won't be around here long." This was his subconscious mind telling him, "All is well."

The commanding officer called him in and informed him that in view of his pre-medical training he was to take an examination; if he received good marks, he would be sent to a medical school at the expense of the Army. He had no trouble passing the examination, and, as a result, shortly began medical training. He now realized that he did not have to go to a particular medical school to be a doctor; he let Infinite Intelligence open the door for him to become what his heart desired.

Prayer Opens Prison Doors

Some years ago I visited a man in prison in New York State. The first thought in his mind was freedom. This prisoner was very bitter and cynical. He had placed himself in prison by his actions against society which were contrary to the golden rule. He was actually living in a psychological prison of hatred and envy. I gave him detailed instructions on how to change his mental attitude. He began to pray for those he hated by affirming frequently, "God's love flows through them, and I wish success and happiness and peace for all of them." He continued to do this many times a day. At night, prior to sleep, he imagined himself at home with his family. He would feel his little daughter in his arms and hear her voice saying, "Welcome,

Daddy." All this was done in his imagination. After a while he made this so real, natural, and vivid that it became a part of him. He had impregnated his subconscious with the belief in freedom.

Another interesting thing happened; he had no further desire to pray for his freedom; this was a sure psychological sign to him that he had embodied the desire for freedom subjectively. He was at peace, and though he was behind bars, he knew subjectively that he was free. It was an inner knowing. Having realized his desire subjectively, he had no further desire to pray about it.

Some weeks passed by, and he was liberated from prison. Friends had come to his rescue, new evidence was submitted on his behalf, and through the proper channels, the door was opened to him for a new life.

Her Prayer Saved Him from Financial Disaster

A young girl who attended my weekly lectures on one of my books, *The Power of Your Subconscious Mind*, stated that there was no way to save her boy-friend from losing his store and suffering ultimate bankruptcy. He could not meet any of his bills; even his automobile was attached. She was saying, "It isn't possible. I see no way out. It is just hopeless."

At my suggestion she reversed this procedure, and three or four times daily she got into a quiet, passive, receptive state of mind. She entered into the mood or feeling that there was a solution for her boy-friend, and nightly went off to sleep dwelling on the following wonderful truth: "I stand still, and I know there is a solution for ———— through the wisdom of my subconscious mind. I accept the way out now and the happy ending in Divine order."

Following the above technique of prayer wherein she rejected mentally all sense-evidence and looked to the wisdom of the subconscious for an answer, her boy-friend called her about a week later and told her a miracle had happened. A check had been presented to him for $2,000 by a man who had borrowed this amount ten years previously. The answer had come out of the blue in response to her prayer of faith. Truly the Bible says, ". . . *Before they call, I will answer; and while they are yet speaking, I will hear.*" (Isaiah 65:24)

Your Daily Prayer

"I know that no matter what the negation of yesterday was, my prayer or affirmation of truth will rise triumphantly over it today.

"Today is God's day; it is a glorious day for me. I am full of peace, harmony, and joy. My faith is in the goodness of God, in the guidance of God, and in the love of God. I am absolutely convinced that my deeper mind receives the impress of my present thoughts now, and I am irresistibly attracting into my experience all the good things my heart desires. I now place all my reliance, faith, and trust in the power and wisdom of God within me; I am at peace.

"I hear the invitation of the God-Presence within me saying, "*Come unto me, all ye that labor . . . and I will give you rest.*" (Matthew 11:28)

"I rest in God; all is well."

POINTS TO REMEMBER

1. Prayer is always the solution. Prayer is a wish turned God-ward, and God answers you.
2. With God all things are possible. God is all-powerful and knows no opposition.
3. Through repetition, faith, and expectancy in the truths of the 91st Psalm, you can lead a charmed life.
4. Complete and utter faith in God can save you from death.
5. Let Divine love and peace enter your heart, and the past will be wiped out and remembered no more.
6. Changed attitudes change everything in your life, and your whole world magically melts in the image and likeness of your dominant conviction.
7. In prayer, ignore your doubts and fears and acknowledge that Infinite Intelligence knows the way out and has the "know-how" of accomplishment.
8. Creative Intelligence, which is God in all men, is no respecter of persons, and It answers all men according to their belief.
9. Prayer opens prison doors when you are living in a psychological prison of hatred, envy, and vengeance.
10. There is always a way. Still the wheels of your mind and be aware that God knows the answer, and because God knows, you know. *"I and my Father are one."* (John 10:30)

11. "*. . . What things soever ye desire, when ye pray,
    believe that ye receive them, and ye shall have them.*"
    (Mark 11:24)

The
Secret Law
of faith

"According to your faith be it unto you."
(Matthew 9:29)

Faith is a way of thinking, an attitude of mind that gets results. The *faith* spoken of in the Bible is a conviction based on eternal laws and principles which never change. Faith is a fusion of your thought and feeling, or your mind and heart, which is so complete, inflexible, and impregnable that no external events or happenings can move you.

In the Eleventh Chapter of Mark you read a marvelous verse, the 23rd, on the power of faith:

> *For verily I say unto you, That whosoever shall say unto this mountain* (your problem, difficulty), *Be thou removed* (that is, eradicated, dissolved), *and be thou cast into the sea* (that means the "sea" of your subconscious, where the healing or solution takes place and problems disappear); *and shall not doubt in his heart* (the heart means your subconscious mind, i.e., your conscious thought and subjective feeling must agree), *but shall believe that those things which he saith shall come to pass; he shall have whatsoever he saith.*

These great truths are very explicit and definitely mean that there is a power and a wisdom within you which can lift you up out of poverty and sickness, reveal to you the answer to your prayer, and set you on the high road to happiness, peace of mind, joy, and harmonious relationship with all people and with the whole world.

Faith-Power Works Wonders

Some years ago a man told me that he was a member of a sales force for a large chemical organization which had two hundred men in the field. The sales manager died, and the vice president offered him the position; however, he turned it down. He realized later that the only reason he rejected the offer was one of fear. He was afraid to attempt the responsibility. This man lacked faith in himself and his inner powers. He hesitated, and a wonderful opportunity passed him by.

During the consultation with this man, I learned that he doubted his ability to succeed. It was Shakespeare who said, "Our doubts are traitors, making us lose the good we oft might win, by fearing to attempt." This man had profound faith in the negative. I explained to him that his faith was completely misplaced. He had faith only in his inadequacy and inability to take promotion and to face life.

He reversed his mental attitude, however, and affirmed boldly: "I am redirecting my thought and feeling; I do not need more faith, I need to use and apply the faith I have in the right way. I know that my subconscious mind reacts according to what I believe about myself. I have faith in the indwelling God, and I know that God is guiding me and directing me, that I was born to succeed, and that Infinite Intelligence reveals to me a new opportunity. I know that I am full of confidence and poise, I have faith in all things good, and I live in the joyous expectancy of the best."

As he began to identify mentally and emotionally with these ideas, he was offered shortly another position in an executive capacity, and he accepted it with alacrity and joy in his heart. This is the magic power of faith.

Everyone Has Faith

Everyone has faith in something. Some have faith in failure, sickness, accidents, and misfortune. When you hear exhortations to have faith, you must remember that you already have faith. The question is, how are you using it—constructively or negatively?

Our mental attitudes and beliefs, which represent our faith, make our own heaven and hell. What is *your* faith? The noblest, grandest, and highest faith is that which is based on eternal principles which never change. Have faith in the creative law of your own mind, in the goodness of God and in all things good, a joyous expectancy of the best, and a firm belief inscribed in your heart that Infinite Intelligence will lead you out of your difficulty and show you the way. Have a firm conviction in the power of God to solve your problems and to heal you. Have faith in the invisible Intelligence within you, which created you and is all-powerful, and which enables you to walk over the waters of fear, doubt, worry, and imaginary dangers of all kinds.

Faith in the Invisible

Paul said, "*Faith is the substance of things hoped for, the evidence of things not seen.*" (Hebrews 11:1)

All great scientists, mystics, poets, artists, and inventors are gifted and are possessed by an abiding faith and trust in the invisible powers within. The scientists and inventors have faith in the possibility of the execution of "the idea." The idea of a radio—though invisible—was real in the mind of the inventor; the idea of an automobile was real in the mind of Henry Ford; the idea of a new structure is real in the mind of the architect. The idea of this book exists in my mind, and all pages are coming forth from the invisible ideas, thoughts, imagery, and beliefs which inhabit my mind.

You must appreciate the fact that your desire, idea, dream, new play, book, script, trip, enterprise, or adventure are all real in your mind, though invisible. To know that your idea is real, that it has form, shape, and substance on the mental plane, and that it is as real as your hand on the objective plane, gives you scientific faith and enables you to walk over the waters of confusion, strife, and fear to a place of conviction deep in your subconscious mind. Whatever is conveyed to your subconscious is projected on the screen of space. This is the way your ideas are objectified.

How His Faith Triumphed

While lecturing in San Francisco some years ago, I interviewed a man who had lost confidence in himself and who was very unhappy and dejected over the way business was going for him. He was the general manager of a large organization. His heart was filled with resentment toward the vice president and the president of the organization. "They oppose me," he claimed. And because of this internal strife, business was declining; he was receiving no dividends and was very frustrated due to lack of faith in himself and in the invisible powers within him.

His statement to me was that he could not believe in that which he could not see, hear, touch, taste, or smell. I asked him, "Can you see your mind, the Life Principle within you, your love for your child, or the thoughts in your mind?" He saw the point and added, "Yes, I know that I am alive and that I can't put life under a microscope or analyze it in a chemical laboratory."

As our conversation progressed, he realized that in order to advance in business and to have peace of mind and success, it was necessary for him to anchor himself to a wisdom and a power which transcended his intellect—that which is substantial and eternal. He decided to unite mentally and emotionally with the inner power lodged in his subconscious mind. This is how he prayed and solved his business problem, applying the following prayer several times daily:

> "All those who work in our corporation are spiritual, wonderful, God-like links in the chain of its growth, welfare, and prosperity. I radiate good will in my thoughts, words, and deeds to my two associates and to all those

in my company. I am full of love and good will for the president and the vice president of our company. Infinite Intelligence makes all decisions through me. There is only right action taking place in my life. I send the thought messengers of peace, love, joy, and harmony before me to the office, and the peace of God reigns supreme in the minds and hearts of all those in the company, including myself. I now go forth into a new day full of faith, confidence, and trust."

This business executive repeated the above prayer slowly four or five times daily, feeling the truth behind the words. He poured life, love, truth, and confidence into the words, and they sank deep down into his subconscious mind. When fearful or angry thoughts came into his mind during the day, he would say, "God's peace fills my soul." After a while, all the harmful thoughts ceased to come, and peace came into his mind.

I later received a letter from this man, saying that at the end of two weeks, the president and the vice president called him into the office, apologized, and each shook hands with him, saying that the organization could not get along without him. His faith was restored, and he knew that, as a conscious individual, with the capability of free choice, he had the power to choose success, harmony, and good will, and to rise above all circumstances and conditions; therefore, he was not under the dominion of externalities nor the impressions of the senses.

She Changed Her Faith

A young girl, who had a special talent in singing, was having great difficulty in getting any work in the motion picture field, television, or radio. She had been turned down so often that she feared she was getting a rejection complex. Speaking to me of her problem, she said, "There are many more beautiful and attractive actresses than I; maybe that's the reason I don't get a contract."

"Well," I replied, "there is a law of mind which points out that supply and demand are one, that what you are seeking is seeking you, and that Infinite Intelligence will direct you to your true place."

She got the idea immediately, and she changed her faith in rejection to faith in acceptance, recognition, and true expression. She began to understand that whatever her mind could imagine and feel to be true, she also could realize.

Twice daily, she quieted the activity of her mind and she removed all tension in her body by simply talking to it and telling it to relax; it has to obey you. In that quiet, receptive, peaceful state, with her attention completely focused on an imaginary movie contract in her hand, she felt the joy and reality of it all. She was definitely mentally and emotionally attached to the contract. She caused the contract to become a reality, and in less than one week she was signed up for a long series of television appearances.

This young woman became identified with the imaginary picture of the contract in her mind, and she knew that what she imagined and believed must come to pass. She changed her mind—her state of faith—and according to her faith was it done unto her.

". . . And calleth those things which be not as though they were." (Romans 4:17)

His Faith Made Him Whole

Some years ago, while giving a series of lectures in Bombay, India, I had a long talk with an Englishman who had great trouble with his legs. He had been confined to his home for nine months, and he walked with great difficulty with the aid of a cane. The first question I asked him was what would he do were he to be healed? He replied, "I would play polo, swim, golf, and climb the Alps, which I used to do every year." That was the answer I was seeking.

I told him in the simplest way possible how to achieve the perfect use of his legs again. The first step was to imagine he was doing the things he ordinarily would do. I suggested that for fifteen or twenty minutes, three times a day, he sit in his study and imagine that he was playing polo; he was to assume the mental mood of actually performing the role of a polo player. In other words, he had to play the role of an actor, as every actor participates in the role he characterizes and dramatizes.

He carried out these instructions carefully. He *felt* himself playing polo. Note carefully that he did not see himself playing polo; that would have been an illusion. He actualized the state by living the drama in his mind. He made it so real and so vivid in his mind that the tangibility of the mallet and the naturalness of the touch of the polo pony became real to him.

At noon he would quiet his mind, still his body, and practically feel his Alpine clothes on him. He would imagine and physically sense he was climbing the Alps; he felt the cold air on his face and heard the voices of his former associates. He lived the drama and felt the solidity and hardness of the rocks.

At night, prior to sleep, he would play an imaginary game of golf. He would hold the club, touch the ball with his hand, put it in place, and tee off. He would swing his club and delight in watching where the ball went. He got into the mood of playing a good game, and he went off to sleep feeling very satisfied and happy about his imaginary experiences of the day.

Within two months this man's legs were healed, and he did all the things he had imagined he would do. Gradually, his imaginary pictures impregnated the deeper layers of his subconscious mind where the healing power is, and there was a reflex action which corresponded to his mental image and feeling. His subconscious mind faithfully reproduced what he had impressed upon it.

Faith Is Your Mind

You are really invisible. Others do not see your motives, feelings, faith, confidence, dreams, aspirations, longings, or the Life Principle within you. When you recall this, you know that you are invulnerable, invincible, eternal, and immortal. You are not a slave of conditions or a victim of circumstance. The Divine Life lives, moves, and has Its being in you, and you live, move, and have your being in this same Divine Life.

Everything in your world is a manifestation of your faith in the unseen. This Omnipotent Presence called God is responsive to your thought and feeling. For example, if you claim, "I am strong and powerful," you will become strong and robust. Your faith is something you *become*, because you manifest and objectify in your world what you really believe about yourself. "*. . . Faith without works is dead.*" (James 2:26) In other words, you will see the works of faith in your mind, body, and affairs. The works of your faith appear in your business or profession, in your home, in the functions of your body, and in all your undertakings. The fruits of faith are health, happiness, peace, love, good will, abundance, security, poise, balance, serenity, and tranquility.

Her Faith in Infinite Intelligence

Recently a girl was wondering whether to accept a position in New York for considerably more money or to remain in Los Angeles in her present position. She quieted her mind and asked herself this question: "What would be my reaction if I made the right decision now?" She said to herself, "I would feel wonderful. I would feel happy, having made the right decision."

"Act as though I am, and I will be." She acted as though she had made the right decision, knowing that the creative Principle of Life is one of love and responsiveness and that It loved her and cared for her. She began to say, "Isn't it wonderful! Isn't it wonderful!" over and over again as a lullaby, and she lulled herself to sleep in the feeling, "It is wonderful."

She had a dream that night, and a voice in the dream said, "Stand still! Stand still!" She awakened immediately, and she knew that it was the inner voice of intuition.

Her subconscious mind had seen all and had known all; it read the minds of the owners of the business in the east. She remained in her present position. Subsequent events proved the truth of her inner voice; the eastern concern went into bankruptcy. "*. . . I the Lord* (the law of your subconscious mind) *will make myself known unto him in a vision, and will speak unto him in a dream.*" (Numbers 12:6)

SERVE YOURSELF WITH FAITH-POWER

1. Faith is an attitude of mind that commands and gets results.
2. You do not need more faith. You have plenty of faith, but you must use it constructively. Give it purposeful direction. Have faith in health, success, peace, and happiness.
3. Everyone has faith in something. Where is your faith? Real faith is based on eternal principles and the values of life which never change.
4. Faith is invisible and is the evidence of things not seen. Scientists have great faith, because they believe in the possibility of the execution of the idea in their mind.
5. You can't see your mind, your life, or your feeling of love. You can't see faith, either, but you can anchor your mind on the invisible Power within you which is substantial and eternal and all-powerful.
6. Change your faith in failure and rejection into faith in acceptance, recognition, and successful living.
7. Have faith in the Healing Power. Imagine and feel that you are now doing all the things you would do were you made whole.
8. Your faith is your mind, and in your deeper mind dwells the omnipotence of God, which responds to your thought and feeling. This is why you can overcome all circumstances and conditions.

9. Mentally act and feel the way you would act and feel were your prayer answered, and you will find that the magic power of faith will work wonders in your life.

The 𝕸iraculous 𝕷aw of healing

There is only *one* healing power. It is called by many names, such as God, Infinite Healing Presence, Nature, Divine Love, Divine Providence, the Miraculous Healing Power, Life, Life Principle, as well as many others. This knowledge goes back into the dim recesses of the past. An inscription has been found written over ancient temples which reads: "The doctor dresses the wound, and God heals the patient."

The healing presence of God is within you. No psychologist, minister, doctor, surgeon, priest, or psychiatrist heals anyone. For example, the surgeon removes a tumor, thereby removing the block and making way for the healing power of God to restore you. The psychologist or psychiatrist endeavors to remove the mental block and encourages the patient to adopt a new mental attitude which tends to release the Healing Presence, flowing through the patient as harmony, health, and peace. The minister asks you to forgive yourself and others and to get in tune with the Infinite by letting the healing power of love, peace, and good will flow through your subconscious mind, thereby cleansing all the negative patterns that may be lodged there.

This infinite healing presence of Life, which Jesus called "Father," is the healing agent in all diseases, whether mental, emotional, or physical.

This miraculous healing power in your subconscious mind, if scientifically directed, can heal your mind, body, and affairs of all disease and impediments. This healing power will respond to you regardless of your race, creed, or color. It does not care whether you belong to any church or whether you have any creedal affiliations or not. You have had hundreds of healings since you were a child. You can recall how this healing presence brought curative results to cuts, burns, bruises, contusions, sprains, etc., and, in all probability, like the author, you did not aid the healing in any way by the application of external remedies.

Healed of Spirit-Voices

A few years ago a young man from a local university came to see me with the complaint that he was constantly hearing spirit-voices, that they made him do nasty things, and that they would not let him alone; neither would they permit him to read the Bible or other spiritual books. He was convinced that he was talking to supernatural beings.

This young man was clairaudient, and, not knowing that all men possess this faculty to some degree, he began to think it was due to evil spirits. His superstitious beliefs caused him to ascribe it to departed spirits. Through constant worry, he became a monomaniac on the subject. His subconscious mind, dominated and controlled by an all-potent but false suggestion, gradually took over control and mastery of his objective faculties, and his reason abdicated its throne. He was what you would call mentally unbalanced, as are all men who allow their false beliefs to obtain the ascendancy.

I explained to this university student that his subconscious mind is of tremendous importance and significance and that it can be influenced negatively and positively, but he had to make sure that he influenced it only positively, constructively, and harmoniously. The subconscious mind possesses transcendent powers, but it is at the same time amenable to good and bad suggestions. The explanation which I gave him made a profound impression on him.

I gave him the following written prayer which he was to repeat for ten or fifteen minutes three or four times a day:

> God's love, peace, harmony, and wisdom flood my mind and heart. I love the truth, I hear the truth, and I know the truth that God is Love, and His love surrounds me, enfolds me, and enwraps me. God's river of peace floods my mind, and I give thanks for my freedom.

He repeated this prayer slowly, quietly, reverently, and with deep feeling, particularly prior to sleep. By identifying himself with harmony and peace, he brought about a rearrangement of the thought-patterns and imagery of his mind, and a healing followed. He brought about a healing of his mind by repetition of these truths, coupled with faith and expectancy.

My own prayer for him night and morning was as follows: "John is thinking rightly. He is reflecting Divine wisdom and Divine intelligence in all his ways. His mind is the perfect mind of God, unchanging and eternal. He hears the voice of God, which is the inner voice of peace and love. God's river of peace governs his mind, and he is full of wisdom, poise, balance, and understanding. Whatever is vexing him is leaving him now, and I pronounce him free and at peace."

I meditated on these truths night and morning, getting the "feel" of peace and harmony; at the end of a week this young man was completely free and at peace.

She Wasn't Expected to Live

Some time ago, a woman told me that her child had a very high fever and was not expected to live. The doctor had prescribed small doses of aspirin and had administered an anti-biotic preparation. The mother, who was involved in a contemplated divorce action, was terribly agitated and emotionally disturbed. This disturbed feeling was communicated subconsciously to the child, and naturally, the child got ill.

Children are at the mercy of their parents and are controlled by the dominant mental atmosphere and emotional climate of those around them. They have not yet reached the age of reason, when they can take control of their own thoughts, emotions, and reactions to life.

The mother, at my suggestion, decided to become more at ease and relax her tensions by reading the 23rd Psalm, praying for guidance and for the peace and harmony of her husband. She poured out love and good will to him and overcame her resentment and inner rage. The fever of the child was due to the suppressed rage and anger of the mother, which was subjectively felt by the child and expressed as a high fever due to the excitation of the child's mind.

Having quieted her own mind, the mother began to pray for her child in this manner: "Spirit, which is God, is the life of my child. Spirit has no temperature; It is never sick or feverish. The peace of God flows through my child's mind and body. The harmony, health, love, and perfection of God are made manifest in every atom of my child's body now. She is relaxed and at ease, poised, serene, and calm. I am now stirring up the gift of God within her, and all is well."

She repeated the above prayer every hour for several hours. Shortly thereafter, she noticed a remarkable change in her child, who awakened and asked for a doll and something to eat. The temperature became normal. What had happened? The fever left the little girl because the mother was no longer feverish or agitated in her mind. Her mood of peace, harmony, and love was instantaneously felt by the child, and a corresponding reaction was produced.

The Natural-Born Healer

We are all "natural-born healers" for the simple reason that the healing presence of God is within all men, and all of us can contact It with our thoughts. It responds to all. This Healing Presence is in the dog, the cat, the tree, and the bird. It is omnipresent and is the life of all things.

Degrees of Faith

There are different degrees of faith. There is the man who, through faith, heals his ulcers, and another who heals a deep-seated, so-called incurable malignancy. It is as easy for the healing presence of God to heal a tubercular lung as it is to heal a cut on your finger. There is no great or small in the God that made us all; there is no big or little, no hard or easy. Omnipotence is within all men. The prayers of the man who lays his hand on another in order to induce a healing simply appeal to the cooperation of the patient's unconscious, whether the latter knows it or not, or whether he ascribes it to Divine intercession or not, and a response takes place; for according to the patient's faith is it done unto him.

A Case of Palsy

An old friend of mine in New York City suffered from palsy and tremors some years ago. His legs would become locked so that inability to move was experienced. Panic would ensue, and my friend would be frozen to the spot, even in the middle of a busy street. He got some mild relief from sedatives and antispasmodics which were prescribed by his physician; however, this condition of constant fear, panic, and foreboding was wearing him down. The following procedure was adopted.

The first step was to get him to see that there was a miraculous healing power within him which had made his body and which also could heal it. I suggested to him that he read the 5th Chapter of Luke, verses 18–24, and a related passage, Mark 2:3–5, where Jesus said to the man with the palsy: *"Man, thy sins are forgiven thee . . . I say unto thee, Arise, and take up thy couch, and go into thine house."*

He read these verses avidly and was deeply moved by them. I explained to him that the couch or bed mentioned in the Bible means the bed in which a man lies in his own mind. The paralyzed man in the Bible undoubtedly was lying down amidst the thoughts of fear, doubt, condemnation, guilt, and superstition. These thoughts paralyze the mind and body.

We are told that Jesus healed the man of palsy by forgiving him his sins. To *sin* is to miss the mark, the goal of health, happiness, and peace. You forgive yourself by identifying mentally and emotionally with your ideal and continuing to do so until it gels within you as a conviction or subjective embodiment. You are sinning also when you think negatively or if you resent, hate, condemn, or engage in fear or worry. You are always sinning when you deviate or turn away from your announced goal or aim in life, which should always be peace, harmony, wisdom, and perfect health—the life more abundant.

My friend admitted to me that he was full of hatred toward a brother who had double-crossed him years ago in a financial deal. He also was full of guilt and self-condemnation and he realized that, like the paralytic in the Bible, he could not be healed until his sins had been cancelled by simply forgiving himself and his brother. He admitted to himself that his physical condition was quite a problem, but that he didn't have to have it.

He turned to the healing presence of God within him and affirmed boldly:

> I fully and freely forgive myself for harboring negative and destructive thoughts, and I resolve to purify my mind from now on. I surrender and release my brother to God, and wherever he is, I sincerely wish for him health, happiness, and all the blessings of God. I am now aligned with the Infinite Healing Power, and I feel Divine love flowing through every atom of my being. I know that God's love is now permeating and saturating my whole body, making me whole and perfect. I sense the peace that passeth understanding. My body is a temple of the living God, and God is in His holy temple and I am free.

As he meditated on these truths, he gradually became reconditioned to health and harmony. As he changed his mind, he changed his body. Changed attitudes change everything. Today he walks joyously and freely, completely healed.

He Healed His Withered Hand

An irate young man came to interview me, stating that his boss had fired him and had said to him, "You're like the man in the Bible with the withered hand." He said to me, "What did he mean? My hands are all right, they are perfectly normal."

My explanation was as follows: In the correct interpretation of the Bible, it must be understood that principles are personified as persons in order to make portrayal and interaction vivid and forceful. We must not confine the story of the man with the withered hand to its literal meaning. The *hand* is a symbol of power, direction, and effectiveness. With your hand, you fashion, mold, direct, and design. Symbolically, a man has a *withered hand* when he has an inferiority complex and feels guilty and inadequate, or is a defeatist. Such a man does not function efficiently and is not expressing his God-given powers.

This young man admitted that his dreams, ambitions, ideals, plans, and purposes were withered and frozen in his mind because he did not know how to bring them to pass. Not knowing the laws of mind and how to pray correctly, he found that his wonderful ideas died a-borning in his mind, resulting in frustration and neurosis. He was stagnating, literally dying on the vine. Furthermore, he was demoting and depreciating himself. His attitude toward life was all wrong; moreover, he admitted that his work was shoddy and desultory.

His hand (his ability to achieve and to accomplish) was withered by saying to himself, "If I had Joe's brains or his wealth . . . his connections . . . I could advance and be somebody. But look at me, just a nobody. I was born on the wrong side of the tracks. I must be satisfied with my lot. I have a withered hand."

A remarkable change took place in this man, however, when he decided to *stretch forth his hand* by enlarging his concept and estimate of himself. He formed a picture in his mind of what he wished to achieve, i.e., to direct a large organization and to be successful. He began to affirm frequently, "I can do all things through the God-power which strengthens, guides, controls, and directs me. I realize that I am going where my vision is. I now turn with faith and confidence to the Infinite Intelligence within me, knowing that I am directed by an inner wisdom. I know in my heart that the God-power flows through the patterns of thought and imagery in my mind, and I am under a Divine compulsion to succeed."

As he identified himself mentally and emotionally with these new concepts, he went forward from promotion to promotion and is now general manager of a large corporation, his current salary exceeding $75,000 annually.

How the Hopeless Case Was Healed

Jesus commanded the dead man, ". . . *And he said, Young man, I say into thee, Arise. And he that was dead sat up, and began to speak.*" (Luke 7:14–15)

When it says *the dead man sat up and began to speak,* it means that when your prayer is answered you speak in a new tongue of joyous health, and you exude an inner radiance. Your dead hopes and desires speak when you bear witness to your inner beliefs and assumptions.

As a corollary to this, I would like to tell about a young man I saw in Ireland a few years ago. He is a distant relative. He was in a comatose condition; his kidneys had not functioned for three days. His condition had been pronounced hopeless when I went to see him, accompanied by one of his brothers. I knew that he was a devout Catholic, and I said to him, "Jesus is right here, and you see him. He is putting his hand out and is this moment laying his hand upon you."

I repeated this several times, slowly, gently, and positively. He was unconscious when I spoke and was not consciously aware of either of us. He sat up in bed, however, opened his eyes, and said to both of us, "Jesus was here; I know I am healed; I shall live."

What had happened? This man's subconscious mind had accepted my statement that Jesus was there, and his subconscious projected that thought-form, i.e., this man's concept of Jesus was portrayed based on what he saw in church statues, paintings, etc. He believed that Jesus was there in the flesh and that he had placed his hands upon him.

The readers of my book, *The Power of Your Subconscious Mind*, are well aware of the fact that you can tell a man who is in a trance that his grandfather is here now and that he will see him clearly. He will see what he believes to be his grandfather. His subconscious reveals the image of his grandfather based on his subconscious memory picture. You can give the same man a post-hypnotic suggestion by saying to him, "When you come out of this trance, you will greet your grandfather and talk to him," and he will do exactly that. This is called a subjective hallucination.

The faith which was kindled in the unconscious of my Catholic relative, based on his *firm belief* that Jesus came to heal him, was the healing factor. It is always done unto us according to our faith, mental conviction, or just blind belief. His subconscious mind was amenable to my suggestion; his deeper mind received and acted upon the idea I had implanted in his mind. In a sense, you could call such an incident *the resurrection of the dead.* It was the resurrection of his health and vitality. According to his belief was it done unto him.

Blind Faith and True Faith

True faith is based on the knowledge of the way your conscious and subconscious minds function and on the combined harmonious functioning of these two levels of mind scientifically directed. Blind faith is healing without any scientific understanding whatsoever of the forces involved. The voodoo doctor or witch doctor in the jungles of Africa heals by faith, and so do the bones of dogs (believed to be the bones of saints by the believer), or anything else which moves man's mind from fear to faith.

In all instances—regardless of the technique, *modus operandi,* process, incantation, or invocation offered to saints and spirits— it is the subconscious mind that does the healing. Whatever you believe is operative instantly in your subconscious mind.

Be like the little eight-year-old boy in our Sunday school. Eye drops were not clearing up his eye infection, and he prayed as follows: "God, you made my eyes. I demand action. I want healing now. Hurry up. Thank you." He had a remarkable healing because of his simplicity, spontaneity, and childlike faith in God. ". . . *Go, and do thou likewise.*" (Luke 10:37)

How to Give a Spiritual Treatment

Spiritual treatment means that you turn to the Indwelling God and remind yourself of His peace, harmony, wholeness, beauty, boundless love, and limitless power. Know that God loves you and cares for you. As you pray this way the fear gradually will fade away. If you pray about a heart condition, do not think of the organ as diseased as this would not be spiritual thinking. Thoughts are things. Your spiritual thought takes the form of cells, tissues, nerves, and organs. To think of a damaged heart or high blood pressure tends to suggest more of what you already have. Cease dwelling on symptoms, organs, or any part of the body. Turn your mind to God and His love. Feel and know that there is only one healing Presence and Power, and to its corollary: *There is no power to challenge the action of God.*

Quietly and lovingly affirm that the uplifting, healing, strengthening power of the healing Presence is flowing through you making you every whit whole. Know and feel that the harmony, beauty, and life of God manifest themselves in you as strength, peace, vitality, wholeness, and right action. Get a clear realization of this, and the damaged heart or other diseased organ will be cured in the light of God's love.

"*. . . Glorify God in your body . . .*" (I Corinthians 6:20)

VERY PROFITABLE POINTERS

1. The healing power of God is within you. Remove any mental block and let the healing power flow through you.

2. A monomaniac is a man who permits his mind to be dominated and controlled by an all-potent but false suggestion.

3. When a mother is agitated and seething with inner turmoil and rage, this negative emotion is communicated to the subconscious of her child and can cause fever. Let God's river of peace flood the mind and heart, and the child's fever will abate and harmony will be restored.

4. All of us are natural-born healers because the Infinite Healing Presence is within us, and we can contact It with our thoughts and beliefs.

5. The miraculous healing power which made your body knows how to heal it. It knows all the processes and functions of your body. Trust the healing power, and accept a healing now.

6. You can recondition yourself to health and harmony as you meditate frequently on harmony, vitality, wholeness, beauty, and perfection.

7. In the Bible, principles are personified as persons in order to make portrayal and interaction vivid and forceful. You can overcome a feeling of inferiority by joining up with God and by sensing that one with God is a majority.

8. There are no incurable diseases. There are incurable people who believe they can't be healed, and according to their belief is it done unto them.

9. Faith healing is healing without any scientific understanding of the forces involved. Spiritual mind healing is the combined and harmonious functioning of your conscious and subconscious mind, scientifically directed for a specific purpose. In all instances, it is the subconscious mind that heals regardless of the technique or process used.

How You Can Face the Word "Incurable" in Your Own Life

Don't let the word "incurable" frighten you. Realize that you are dealing with the Creative Intelligence which made your body and that, although some men will say that a healing is impossible, be assured that this infinite Healing Presence is instantly available, and you can always draw on its power through the creative law of your own mind. Make use of this power now and perform miracles in your life. Remember that a miracle cannot prove that which is impossible; it is a confirmation of that which is possible, for "... *with God all things are possible.*" (Matthew 19:26) "... *I will restore health unto thee, and I will heal thee of thy wounds, saith the Lord ...*" (Jeremiah 30:17)

The word "Lord" in the Bible means the creative law of your mind. There is a deep-lying, healing principle which permeates the entire universe, that flows through your mental patterns, images, and choices, and objectifies them in form. You can bring into your life anything you wish through this infinite healing principle which operates through your own mind.

You may use this universal healing principle for any particular purpose. It is not confined to healing of the mind or body. It is the same principle which attracts to you the ideal husband or wife, prospers you in business, finds for you your true place in life, and reveals answers to your most difficult problems. Through the correct application of this principle, you can become a great salesman, musician, physician, or surgeon. You can use it to bring harmony where discord exists, peace to supplant pain, joy in place of sadness, and abundance in place of poverty.

Healing of Dropsy

I knew a man in London, England, who was not only very religious but was completely free from any ill will or resentment. However, he saw his father die of dropsy, and it made a very deep and lasting impression on him; he told me that all his life since that event he feared that the same thing would happen to him. He also told me that his father by way of treatment used to be tapped with an instrument, and that the doctor would draw out large amounts of water from his abdominal area. This lingering fear, which was never neutralized, was undoubtedly the cause of his dropsical condition. He did not know the simple psychological truth which Dr. Phineas Parkhurst Quimby of Maine had elucidated about one hundred years ago. Dr. Quimby said that *if you believe something, it will manifest, whether you are consciously thinking of it or not.* This man's fear grew into a conviction that he would become a victim of the same disorder that had troubled his father. This explanation, however, helped the man considerably. He began to realize that he had accepted a lie as truth.

I pointed out to him that his fear was a perversion of the truth, a fear which had no real power because there is no principle behind disease. There is a principle of health, none of disease; a principle of abundance, none of poverty; a principle of honesty, none of deceit; a principle of mathematics, none of error; and a principle of beauty, none of ugliness. Fortunately, his belief was in the only power which controlled him, and he knew that his mind could be used negatively or positively.

He came to a definite conclusion in his mind by reasoning that the Healing Presence which made him was still with him and that his disease was due to a disordered group of disease-soaked thoughts; thus he rearranged his mind to conform to the Divine pattern of harmony, health, and wholeness.

Before going to sleep at night, he would affirm with feeling and with deep meaning behind each word: "The Healing Presence is now going to work, transforming, healing, restoring, and controlling all processes of my body according to Its wisdom and Divine nature. My entire system is cleansed, purified, and quickened by the vitalizing energy of God. Divine circulation, assimilation, and elimination operate in my mind and body. The joy of the Lord is my abiding strength. I am made every whit whole, and I give thanks."

He repeated this prayer every night for about thirty days. At the end of that time, his mind had reached a conviction of health, and his physician dismissed him as whole and perfect.

Steps in Healing

The first step in healing is not to be afraid of the manifest condition—from this very moment. The second step is to realize that the condition is only the product of past thinking, which will have no more power to continue its existence. The third step is mentally to exalt the miraculous healing power of God within you.

This procedure instantly will stop the production of all mental poisons in you or in the person for whom you are praying. Live in the embodiment of your desire, and your thought and feeling will soon be made manifest. Do not allow yourself to be swayed by human opinion and worldly fears, but live emotionally in the belief that it is God in action in your mind and body.

Spiritual Blindness

Millions of people are "blind," i.e., they are psychologically and spiritually "blind" because they do not know that they become what they think all day long. Man is spiritually and mentally "blind" when he is hateful, resentful, or envious of others. He does not know that he is actually secreting mental poisons which tend to destroy him.

Thousands of people are constantly saying that there is no way to solve their problems, and their situation is hopeless. Such an attitude is the result of spiritual blindness. Man begins to see spiritually and mentally when he gets a new understanding of his mental powers, and develops a conscious awareness that the wisdom and intelligence in his subconscious can solve all his problems.

Everyone should become aware of the interrelationship and interaction of the conscious and subconscious mind. Persons who were once *blind* to these truths, after careful introspection, will now begin to *see* the vision of health, wealth, happiness, and peace of mind that can be theirs through the correct application of the laws of mind.

Vision Is Spiritual, Eternal, and Indestructible

We do not create vision, rather we manifest or release it. We see *through* the eye, not *with* it. The cornea of the eye is stimulated by light waves from objects in space; through the optic nerve, these stimuli are carried to the brain. When the inner light, or intelligence, meets the outer light in this manner, by a process of interpretation, we see.

Your eyes symbolize Divine love and a delight in the ways of God, plus a hunger and thirst for God's truth. Your *right eye* symbolizes right thought and right action. The *left eye* symbolizes God's love and wisdom. Think right and radiate good will to all, and you will focus perfectly.

> . . . *Receive thy sight . . . And immediately he received his sight, and followed him, glorifying God . . .* (Luke 18:42–43)

Special Prayer for Eyes and Ears

> I am the Lord that healeth me. My vision is spiritual, eternal, and a quality of my consciousness. My eyes are Divine ideas, and they are always functioning perfectly.

My perception of spiritual Truth is clear and powerful. The light of understanding dawns in me; I see more and more of God's Truth every day. I see spiritually; I see mentally; I see physically. I see images of Truth and Beauty everywhere.

The infinite Healing Presence is now, this moment, rebuilding my eyes. They are perfect, Divine instruments, enabling me to receive messages from the world within and the world without. The glory of God is revealed in my eyes.

I hear the Truth; I love the Truth; I know the Truth. My ears are God's perfect ideas, functioning perfectly at all times. My ears are the perfect instruments which reveal God's harmony to me. The love, beauty, and harmony of God flow through my eyes and ears; I am in tune with the Infinite. I hear the still, small voice of God within me. The Holy Spirit quickens my hearing, and my ears are open and free.

STEP THIS WAY FOR A HEALING

1. Man says it's impossible, but with God all things are possible. You can be healed by God, Who created you.
2. The healing principle flows through your mental patterns of thought and imagery, bringing all things you wish into manifestation.
3. If you believe something, it will be manifest—whether or not you are consciously thinking of it. Believe only in that which heals, blesses, and inspires you.
4. Exalt the power of God in the midst of you, and you will stop the spread of any disease in your body.
5. The thankful heart is close to God. Let all your prayers be made known with praise and thanksgiving.
6. You are spiritually blind when you don't know that thoughts are things, that what you feel you attract, and that what you imagine, you become.
7. Vision is spiritual, eternal, and indestructible. A wonderful prayer for the eyes is to affirm regularly: "I see better spiritually, mentally, and physically."
8. *"I will lift up mine eyes unto the hills, from whence cometh my help."* (Psalm 121:1)

The
Dynamic Law
of protection

I had occasion some time ago to visit a woman in the Post Graduate Hospital in New York who was suffering from cancer. The woman confessed to me that for thirty years she had hated her daughter-in-law "like poison," to use her own expression. She said that she had never thought of cancer or feared it—which was probably true—but her destructive, poisonous emotion toward her daughter-in-law had become lodged in her subconscious mind and had taken the form of cancer in her body. Following my advice, she began to practice the great art of forgiveness by whole-heartedly, sincerely, and lovingly praying for her daughter-in-law, mentioning her name, as follows:

The peace of God fills her soul; she is inspired and blessed in all her ways. God is prospering her, and I rejoice that the Law of God is working for her, through her, and all around her. I feel in my heart and soul that I have released her, and whenever the thought of her enters my mind, I wish her well. I am now free.

This woman's spirit of forgiveness, together with cobalt and other medical treatment which she received, brought about a remarkable change in her personality, and a wonderful healing took place. Her prayer changed her subconscious mind by eliminating and neutralizing all the negative patterns lodged therein, and its embodiment also had to disappear.

A New Concept of God Works Wonders

A few months ago, I spent some time in the home of a very kind man. He was noble, generous, and magnanimous in every way. He had cancer, however, in the same organ of his body as had his father and two brothers, all of whom died from cancer of the prostate gland. This man had feared he would have cancer in the same organ, and he commented that he had lived with that fear for over twenty years. Job said, "The thing I greatly feared has come upon me."

When this man prayed, he really was begging some far-off God, saying, "If it is God's will, He will heal me." Here again was the old jungle concept of an avenging God punishing his children. This man, after hearing a new concept of God, now has acquired an optimistic, cheerful outlook on life, and he is receiving encouragement and praise from his physician. As he changed his conscious mind's belief, it was automatically communicated to his subconscious mind, which responded accordingly.

The Cause Is Mental

Most people, when they read about train accidents, auto disasters, etc., seem to think that some outside force comes from somewhere and does harm to people who are entirely innocent; but the mental state and the disasters are "birds of a feather," and they "flock together."

How to Protect Yourself

A man who possesses a strong faith, trusting that an Overshadowing Providence always is watching over him, is kept away from an unpleasant experience that might hurt or injure him in the same manner that oil and water repel one another. Man's faith in God and His love, and the unpleasant experience repel one another according to the law of belief.

Become Invulnerable

Affirm regularly and systematically: *"He that dwelleth in the secret place of the most High shall abide under the shadow of the Almighty. I will say of the Lord, He is my refuge and my fortress: my God; in him will I trust."* Ps. 91:1–2.

Believe these truths in your heart, and you positively will be invulnerable against all misfortune. You will have nothing at all to fear in the world. There is a mental attitude and a mental cause behind all accidents, fires, wars, and calamities of all kinds. Man is cause; he is also effect.

Why She Had No Boy-Friends

A young girl from Wyoming, who is working in an office in Los Angeles, said to me: "I am very shy, timid, and hesitant, and I have no boy-friends." She wanted to be married and have a home of her own, to love and to be loved, and to be called "Mrs. Jones."

I explained to her how to realize her desires. Actually, by her mental attitude, she was rejecting her good.

She decided to feel that she was wanted, cared for, and admired. She purchased a date book in a ten-cent store and placed the names of imaginary admirers in the book. Then she began to imagine that she was so popular with men that she could say "no" after looking up the names in the book. All this was done in her imagination at night and at other times during the day. She soon became immensely popular with men and was no longer a wallflower.

This young woman decided to marry [5] and claimed that Infinite Intelligence was attracting to her an ideal companion, who would harmonize with her perfectly. She imagined a wedding ring on her finger at night as she went to sleep. She would mentally "touch" and "feel" the ring. She actualized the state and impregnated her subconscious mind by feeling the naturalness, solidity, and tangibility of the ring; moreover, she said that the ring implied to her that the marriage already was consummated and that she was resting in the accomplished fact. She eventually attracted a most wonderful man, and today they blend harmoniously in every way.

---

[5] *The Power of Your Subconscious Mind*, page 151: "How to Attract the Ideal Husband," Joseph Murphy, Prentice-Hall, Inc., Englewood Cliffs, New Jersey, 1963.

How He Became the Best Student

A father was fearful and worried about the future of his son. The boy's teacher said the child was dull, stupid, and backward, and that he should be sent to a special school. The father on my advice began to get lost in the joy of hearing the opposite. Every night he imagined that his son was showing him a report card and was saying, "Daddy, I received all A's!"

He continued this imagery until it penetrated his subconscious and became a living conviction. His boy responded beautifully and blossomed forth as one of the best students in his class. The father experienced the fruit of the idea on which he had meditated. The father's prayer caused the intelligence and wisdom of the subconscious to well up in the mind of the boy, and he fulfilled his father's conviction of him.

He Could Not Be Shot

I chatted with a young Japanese man during a series of lectures a few years ago in Japan. He told me that he had been sentenced to be shot during the war; he added, though, that he had been falsely accused, but that is beside the point, at this time. While in prison, he kept repeating silently to himself the words of the 91st Psalm. Prior to sleep every night, he would say to his deeper mind, "I can't be shot. I am God's son, and God can't shoot Himself."

This man knew there was but One Power and One Life, and that his life was God's Life. He told me that subsequently he was released with no explanation and ordered back to duty. This young man wrote his freedom in his subconscious mind by reiterating the truths of the Psalm and by picturing his freedom.

Whatever you impregnate your subconscious with, it responds accordingly.

Your Answer Determines Your Future

When I was a boy, I used to listen to my uncles and aunts conversing about many things. Often, they would say, "You know, John or Mary met with that accident because he or she ceased going to church." Whenever any calamity came to people, somehow they were considered sinful and the object of the wrath or the will of God.

I often wondered what kind of a God they had in their minds. What is your concept of God? Do you know that the answer you give to that question inevitably determines your whole future?

Your Belief About God Really Is Your Belief About Yourself

If you think that God is cruel, vindictive, and an inscrutable, tyrannical, cannibalistic Moloch in the skies, a sort of oriental sultan or despot punishing you, of course, you will experience the result of this habitual thinking, and your life will be hazy, confused, and full of fear and limitations of all kinds. In other words, you will experience the results of the nature of your belief about God. You actually will have negative experiences because of your belief.

God becomes to you whatever you consider Him to be. Above all things, get the right concept of God. It makes no difference what you call God. You may call Him Allah, Brahma, Vishnu, Reality, Infinite Intelligence, The Healing Presence, The Oversoul, Divine Mind, The Architect of the Universe, The Supreme

Being, The Life Principle, The Living Spirit, or The Creative Power. The point is, your belief or conviction about God governs and gives direction to your whole life.

Believe in a God of Love

Millions of people believe in a God that sends sickness, pain, and suffering; they believe in a cruel and vindictive Deity. They do not have a good God, and, to them, God is not a loving God. Having such weird, ignorant concepts of God, they experience the results of their beliefs in the form of all kinds of difficulties and troubles. Your subconscious mind manifests your beliefs and projects them as experiences, conditions, and events.

Your nominal belief about God is meaningless. The thing that matters is your real, subconscious belief—the belief of your heart. You always will demonstrate your belief; that is why Dr. Quimby said one hundred years ago, "Man is belief expressed." Millions of people conceive of a God of caprice, afar-off in the skies, who possesses all the whims of a human being. With such a concept, they are like the businessman who once said to this writer, "I would be all right if God would leave me alone." Believe that God is love, that He watches over you and cares for you, and that He guides, prospers, and loves you, and wonders will happen in your life which transcend your fondest dreams!

Becoming a New Man

> . . . *His name shall be called Wonderful, Counsellor, the mighty God, The everlasting Father, The Prince of Peace.* (Isaiah 9:6)

Begin now, today, as you read these lines, to enthrone the above true concept or belief about God, and miracles will begin to happen in your life. Realize and know that God is all bliss, joy, indescribable beauty, absolute harmony, infinite intelligence, and boundless love, and that He is omnipotent, supreme, and the only Presence.

Accept mentally that God is all these things as unhesitatingly as you accept the fact that you are alive; then you will begin to experience in your life the wonderful results of your new conviction about the blessed God within you. You will find your health, your vitality, your business, your environment, and the world in general all changing for the better. You will begin to prosper spiritually, mentally, and materially. Your understanding and spiritual insight will grow in a wonderful way, and you will find yourself transformed into a new man.

His Business Prospered 300%

A businessman in London, England, said to me after a lecture, "I have feared poverty all my life; what can I do?" I told him to look upon God as his silent partner, his guide, and his counsellor, to believe that God always was watching over him like a loving father, and to claim boldly that God was supplying all his needs and inspiring him in all his ways.

He wrote to me a few months later, saying, "I feel God is a Living Presence, a friend, a counsellor, and a guide. My business has prospered three hundred per cent, my health is better, and I have thrown away the thick lenses I wore for twenty years!"

You can see what happened when this man decided to look upon God as his Father. The word *father* meant something to him. It meant love, protection, guidance, and supply. Let wonders happen the same way in your life.

The Miracle of Three Steps

In the course of my ministry I performed a marriage ceremony for a wonderful young couple in the Midwest. After about a month, however, they separated, and the wife returned to her parents' home. What had happened to their romance?

While talking with the young man later, he said to me, "Every day I kept thinking that she would run around with other men. I was jealous of her. I did not trust her. I imagined that she was with former boy friends, and I was full of fear that I would lose her."

The young man was imagining evil about his wife and was co-habiting mentally with fear, jealousy, and loss. He had broken his marriage vows, wherein he had promised to cherish, love, and honor her at all times, and, forsaking all others, to remain faithful to her alone. This young man's fear was communicated to the subconscious mind of his wife, who was not acquainted with the laws of mind, and so, in the course of events, what he feared and believed actually took place. He saw his belief made manifest; then he blamed his wife. In truth, however, it was done unto him as he believed.

When this young couple learned about the workings of their conscious and subconscious mind, through my presentation in one of my books, *The Power of Your Subconscious Mind*, they began to pray together each night and morning and to practice the miracle of three steps, as follows:

The first step: In the beginning, God. The moment they awakened in the morning, they claimed God was guiding them in all their ways. They sent out loving thoughts of peace, harmony, and joy to each other and to the whole world.

The second step: They said grace at breakfast. They gave thanks for the wonderful food, for their abundance, and for *all* of their blessings. They made sure that no problems, worries, or arguments entered into their table conversation; the same applied at dinner time.

The third step: They alternated in praying aloud each night. They kept their Bible close at hand and read a selection from it prior to sleep, such as the 23rd, 91st, and 27th Psalms, the eleventh chapter of Hebrews, and the thirteenth chapter of First Corinthians. They said quietly, "Thank you, Father, for all the blessings of the day. God giveth His beloved sleep."

Each one decided to stop doing the things which irritated the other. This took discipline plus an intense desire on both sides to "make a go" of their marriage. As they followed this down-to-earth procedure, harmony eventually was restored to them.

The Couple Was Re-United

I had rather a strange interview one time with a man and woman who came to see me at my hotel in Dallas, Texas. They were both worried and anxious over their actions. They said they had quarreled over a piece of property a few years previously. They had been very angry toward one another, and each had sued for divorce. They were divorced after about a year of litigation, and each of them had remarried. However, they said it was all a great mistake. They had married on what they called the rebound. They said, "We still love each other. What shall we do?"

I advised them to dissolve the sham and farce of their present marriages and to go back to each other. They realized that they had been living a lie with their present spouses, and that this was not just or fair, because no real love prevailed.

These two people were teachable and humble in that they admitted their mistake, which could be called foolish pride plus a desire to get even with one another. They allowed the inner love in their hearts for one another to lead them back to the Altar of Love. The "rebound" marriages were dissolved amicably, and all those involved were blessed thereby. The couple were re-united.

Love binds two hearts together, and it is an indissoluble link. "Whom God (Love) hath joined together, let no man put asunder."

The Transforming Power of Love

I was asked recently if a father, by mental means, could break up or cause the dissolution of a marriage. The young lady in question is married to a Catholic; she and her husband are deeply in love. "My father," she said, "hates Catholics, and he belongs to another church."

The father had his daughter in a state of fright, and she was terrified that he could get her back by mental means.

I explained to her that her father had no power whatsoever, no more than a rabbit's foot or the stones in a field. She began to realize that the only real power existed in her own thought and feeling. She prayed frequently that as God's love united her with her husband in the beginning, His love would continue to unite them now, surrounding them and enfolding them. The young woman affirmed regularly that the beauty, love, and harmony of God permeated their minds and hearts and that God's love ruled their lives. She realized that nothing could come between her and the man she loved.

She perceived a great truth, which is that all the negative statements and thoughts of others are as papier-mâché arrows aimed at a battleship. Love is of the heart, and as this young husband and wife found love, grace, and good will in one another, and saw the virtues of the other, their marriage grew more blessed every day. The young woman prayed for Divine understanding with her father, and she informed me recently that he was becoming more tolerant now and was learning to love her husband.

Prayer Transformed a Criminal

I once visited a man who was on his deathbed. He was a chronic alcoholic and had committed various crimes, and he found himself at the end of the rope. He related to me all his crimes and asked me if he would be punished by God and go to hell when he died.

I explained to this desperate man that God punishes no one, but that by our misuse of the laws of life we punish ourselves, either through ignorance or by wilfully violating the laws of harmony, love, and right action. I added that he had to forgive himself and let God's love enter his soul, and that he must resolve to be a new man in God; then the past would be wiped out and remembered no more.

We prayed together, and he appeared radiant and happy after the prayer. The reason for this was that he now had a deep inner faith and conviction that he was on the right side of God and that all was forgiven. He was very relaxed and said he was ready for what he called "Heaven." His doctor noticed a remarkable improvement in the man, and shortly thereafter the prognosis was made that he would live. Indeed, within ten days he left the hospital, whole and healthy again!

The man is now eighty-five years old and still is very strong and healthy. He has become a wonderful, upright, God-like man—completely transformed. How did all this come about? It was the result of his acceptance of the truth about God and his complete surrender of all his crimes, hates, and guilt which immediately released his mind and body. His body responded in a miraculous manner to his new mental attitude. His inner sense of freedom and peace of mind—nothing else—was the healing agent.

Prayer Saved His Life

A man in a hospital was suffering from acute septicaemia, for which he had received antibiotics and several transfusions. No improvement was observed. He was on the critical list and not expected to live. He said to me while discussing his former business associate, "I loathe that man," and, "He did me dirt." His loathing had become a festering psychic wound. He told me he was afraid that when he was discharged from the hospital he would get a gun and murder the man.

I pointed out to this very ill man that he was in reality murdering *himself*. Although he would not associate with the man who had double-crossed and swindled him, he was entertaining him constantly in his mind, in his blood stream, in his brain, and in the very marrow of his bones, where his blood is generated. I explained that he was giving the man power over his own mind, body, and all his vital organs.

He perceived the truth that the other man was not responsible for his sickness, inasmuch as he is the *only thinker in his universe* and therefore responsible for the thoughts, concepts, and images that he entertained. I gave him a prayer formula to meditate on, which prayer will be found in the closing section of this chapter. He had a rapid recovery from his blood dyscrasia as he saturated his mind with the truths of God. Truly, wonders happen as you pray!

The Power of God

Following is a prayer which has helped numerous people to completely transform their lives. As you meditate on these wonderful truths, you, too, will shortly discover that wonders are happening in your life!

> God is the only Presence and the only Power, and I am one with It. God's strength is my strength; His Intelligence floods my mind. This new awareness gives me complete dominion in every department of my life. I am now joined to the One Universal Mind, which is God. His wisdom, power, and glory flow through me. I know that the energy and power of God permeate every atom, tissue, muscle, and bone of my being, making me perfect now. God is Life, and this Life is my life. My faith is renewed; my vitality is restored. God walks and talks in me. He is my God; I am one with Him. His Truth is my shield and buckler; I rejoice that it is so. Under His wings shall I trust. I dwell in the Secret Place of the Most High, and I abide under the Shadow of the Almighty.

POINTS TO REMEMBER

1. Hatred is a mental poison. Forgiveness and love are the spiritual antidotes to use, and then a healing follows.
2. Get a new concept of God as Love. Realize that God is *for* you—not against you.
3. Your mental attitude is cause, and your experience is effect.
4. You can protect yourself from all harm by realizing that God's Love surrounds you, enfolds you, and enwraps you.
5. Believe in your heart the truths expounded in the 91st Psalm, and you will be invulnerable.
6. Imagine and feel that you are loved, wanted, and appreciated, and you will never lack friends.
7. Pray for the so-called backward child by calling forth in prayer and meditation the intelligence and wisdom of God, which is inherent in all children.
8. Mentally write your freedom in your subconscious mind, and it will respond accordingly.
9. Your real belief about God determines your whole fate.
10. Your belief about God is your real belief about yourself. "Man is belief expressed." (Quimby)
11 Your nominal belief about God is meaningless. What really matters is the belief in your heart.
12. Believe that God is all bliss, peace, beauty, joy, and love, and that what is true of God is true of you.

Make a habit of this, and wonders will happen in your life!

13. Boldly claim that God supplies all your needs, and you will prosper in all your ways.

14. Your habitual fears can be communicated to the subconscious of your spouse. Form a habit of thinking on that which is lovely and of good report.

15. When God's love unites a husband and wife, no person, place, or condition can break up the marriage. Love is the indissoluble link which binds.

16. God, or Life, punishes no one. We punish ourselves, either through ignorance or by wilfully violating the the laws of harmony, love, and right action.

17. Hatred is a deadly poison, causing the death of all the vital organs of the body.

The Mysterious Law of inner guidance

When you are perplexed, confused, and fearful, and wonder what decision to make, remember that you have an *inner guide* that will lead and direct you in all your ways, revealing to you the perfect plan, and showing you the way you should go. The secret of guidance or right action is to mentally devote yourself to the right answer until you find its response within you.

The infinite intelligence deep in your subconscious mind is responsive to your request. This response you will recognize as an inner feeling, an awareness, an overpowering hunch leading you to the right place at the right time, putting the right words into your mouth, and causing you to do the right thing in the right way.

Follow the Lead Which Comes

A minister friend of mine once asked me whether I thought the governing board of the church which he directed should purchase another church property presently being vacated. I answered, "Let's pray about it and follow the *lead* that comes."

Nothing happened for a few days; then he phoned me and said they were having a board meeting to decide whether or not to purchase the property. While he was talking, I could *feel* that the answer was "No," and he said that the same intuitive feeling of "No" was felt also by him. Subsequent events proved that he was right.

There Always Is an Answer

A radio listener wrote to me, saying that one of her tenants had been boisterous, rude, noisy, and frequently had drunken brawls in his apartment, annoying all the other tenants. He refused to leave. However, she stilled her mind and prayed that the infinite intelligence in the subconscious mind of her tenant would guide and direct him to his true place and would prompt him to leave in peace and harmony at once. She affirmed boldly, "I release him completely. I loose him and let him go, wishing for him peace, love, and happiness."

She had continued to pray in this manner until she got the reaction which satisfied, which means inner peace and tranquility. The man suddenly paid his rent up and quietly left. She subsequently attracted a very spiritual-minded tenant.

A Businessman's Guidance Formula

A businessman recently related to me how he prays for guidance. He has a rather simple technique. He goes into his private office in the morning where he is not disturbed, closes his eyes, and thinks of the attributes and qualities of God which he knows are all within him; this generates a mood of peace, power, and confidence. Then he speaks in the following simple manner to the Father within Who doeth the works: "Father, thou knowest all things. Give me the idea necessary for a new program." He then imagines that he has the answer and that it is flowing through his mind. He affirms, "I accept the answer, and I give thanks for it now."

After this prayer, he gets busy and becomes preoccupied with routine matters, and the answer inevitably reveals itself when he is not thinking about it. He said that often the answers come like a flash, spontaneously and unannounced. The amazing suddenness with which the solutions to his business problems come sometimes is startling, indeed.

Professor Gets Specific Answer

A college professor who attends my public lectures needed specific data for his book, the research dating back to perhaps 1000 or 1500 B.C. He said that he didn't know exactly where to find it; he thought it might be in the British Museum 8000 miles away, or in the New York Public Library 3000 miles away. He believed that it would take him days and possibly even weeks to find it. Furthermore, he didn't know exactly what to ask for when confronted by the librarian.

I suggested to him that in such an instance, he should relax and be still, and say silently and quietly prior to sleep, "My subconscious knows the answer, and it gives me all the information I need." Then he was to drop off to sleep with the one word, "answer," in his mind. In that relaxed mood, he simply repeated over and over the word, "answer."

Your subconscious mind is all-wise, knows what type of answer you need, and will answer in a dream, as an overpowering hunch, or a feeling that you are being led on the right track. You may get a sudden flash of intuition to go to a certain place, or another person may give you the answer.

He practiced the above technique for a few nights, and on the morning of the third day, on his way to college, he had an intense desire to visit an old book store downtown. The minute he entered the book store, and on looking over the books on display near the door, he picked up the very book that gave him all the desired data.

Be On the Qui Vive

Sometimes, we get impressions as Divine guidance, and we must be on the lookout or *qui vive* for them. When a feeling or idea comes to us, we must recognize it and follow it.

Be Still and Relaxed

There are two reasons why we do not acknowledge our inner guidance. These are tension and failure to recognize the lead when it comes. If we are in a happy, confident, joyous mood, we will recognize the flashes of intuition that come to us. Moreover, we will feel under subjective compulsion to carry them out.

Therefore, it is necessary to be still and relaxed when you pray for guidance, as nothing can be achieved by tenseness, fear, or apprehension. Your subconscious mind answers you when your conscious mind is still, receptive, and relaxed.

She Gets Wonderful Slogans

Here is how one young lady in the advertising business produces her wonderful slogans: She drops off to sleep with the words "right slogan" on her lips, knowing that the answer will be forthcoming—and it always is. *"He faileth not."* (Zephaniah 3:5)

Intuition Pays Fabulous Dividends

The word "intuition" means taught from within. Intuition goes much farther than reason. You employ reason to carry out intuition. Intuition is the spontaneous answer that wells up from your subconscious mind in response to your conscious thinking.

For business and professional people, the cultivation of the intuitive faculty is of paramount importance. Intuition offers instantaneously that which the intellect or reasoning mind of man could accomplish only after weeks or months of monumental trial and error.

When our reasoning faculties fail us in our perplexities, the intuitive faculty sings the silent song of triumph. The conscious mind of man is reasoning, analytical, and inquisitive; the subjective faculty of intuition always is spontaneous. It comes as a beacon to the conscious intellect. Many times it speaks as a warning against a proposed trip or plan of action.

How a Novelist Gets Marvelous Ideas

I once chatted with a wonderful novelist in Calcutta who told me that the secret of her success in writing was due to the fact that she regularly and systematically claimed that God was guiding her in all her ways and that she would astonish the world with the beauties, glories, and gems of wisdom given to her by God within her.

Her favorite prayer was: "God knows all things. God is my Higher Self, the Spirit in me. God is writing a novel through me. He is giving me the theme, the characters and their names, and the locations and setting. He reveals the ideal drama in perfect sequence. I give thanks for the answer which I know is coming, and I go off to sleep with the word 'novel' on my lips, until I am lost in the deep of sleep."

This novelist knew that the word "novel" would be etched on her subconscious mind and that the latter would respond. She said that usually, after praying this way prior to writing a novel, a few days later she would get the inner urge to write, and the words and scenes would flow in an unending stream.

This is representative of the miracle of Divine guidance which is available to us all.

He Found His True Place

A salesman said to me, "I'm a square peg in a round hole! I go from job to job. Isn't there a right place for me?"

I helped him to see that there was an answer to his problem, because the infinite intelligence and wisdom of his subconscious mind knew his talents and also knew how to open the door for his perfect expression in life. I directed him to pray as follows: "I believe and accept without question that there is a creative intelligence in my subconscious mind which knows all and sees all. I know that I am directed rightly to my true place in life. I accept this inner guidance without question. I am here for a purpose, and I am willing to fulfill that purpose now."

He left my office in a very happy mood, and within a few

days' time he obtained an ideal position. His inner guide had directed him to the right place, had caused him to say the right words, and to make the correct impression.

A Prayer for Divine Guidance

I know that there is a perfect law of supply and demand. My motives are right, and I desire to do the right thing in the right way at all times. I am instantly in touch with everything I need. I am in my true place now; I am giving of my talents in a wonderful way, and I am Divinely blessed. Infinite Intelligence is guiding me now in thought, word, and deed, and whatever I do is controlled by God and by God alone. I am a perfect channel of God.

I feel, know, and believe that my God-Self illumines my pathway. Divine Intelligence inspires, directs, and governs me in all my undertakings and instantaneously reveals to me the answer to all things I need to know. Divine love goes before me, making all roads a highway of peace, love, joy, and happiness. It is wonderful!

IDEAS TO REMEMBER

1. Mentally and emotionally devote yourself to the right answer, and you will get a response.
2. Infinite Intelligence in your subconscious mind knows all and sees all. Call upon It and you will receive an answer. It knows only the answer.
3. Follow the *lead* which comes. Often, it flashes spontaneously into your conscious mind like toast pops out of a toaster.
4. Remember that there always is an answer. Persevere and relax, and you will perceive wonders happening when you pray.
5. Praying for guidance is a two-way conversation. Ask your deeper mind for the answer with faith and confidence, and you will get an answer.
6. Your subconscious mind answers you in ways you know not of. You may be led to a bookstore and pick up a book which answers your question, or you may overhear a conversation which provides the solution to your problem. The answers may come in countless ways.
7. It is necessary to be alert, alive, and on the *qui vive*, so that you will recognize the lead which comes— and then follow it.
8. The wisdom of your subconscious rises to your surface mind, or conscious mind, when the latter is relaxed and at peace. Relaxation is the key.
9. Drop off to sleep with the word "answer" on your

lips, repeating it over and over again as a lullaby, and the appropriate answer will be given you.

10. You use your intellect to carry out the voice of intuition.

11. If you are a novelist or a writer, claim that the wisdom of your subconscious is revealing to you the theme and characters, prompting you in all ways. You will be amazed at the results.

12. Infinite Intelligence within you will guide you to your true place and reveal your hidden talents.

13. Affirm, "Divine love goes before me, making straight, joyous, glorious, and happy my ways," and all your ways will be ways of pleasantness and all your roads will be paths of peace.

The
𝕸ighty 𝕷aw
of courage

You can
learn to live so that fear will no longer dominate you, although your fear may reach back into the past, maybe even
into the inheritance of the race mind. While there are many
primitive fears in the subconscious of all of us, you can eradicate all those fears by joining mentally and emotionally with
the God-Presence within you. As you learn to love God and
all things good and as you trust Him implicitly, you will overcome your fears and become a free and fearless person.

How Prayer Freed Her from Panic

A few years ago, a girl named Anne, whom I did not know,
phoned me at the Algonquin Hotel in New York City, saying,

"My father died. I know he has hidden a large sum of money in the house. I am panic-stricken, desperate, and full of fear; I need the money and I can't find it."

She did not know how to communicate with her subconscious mind, and I told her that I would pray about it. I asked her to visit me the next day.

That same night following her phone call I had a dream in which a man said, "Get up and write this down; you are seeing my daughter, Anne, tomorrow." I awoke and went to the desk and rustled through the drawer for a sheet of hotel stationery. He dictated to me as I wrote. I am sure that these instructions were not written by Joseph Murphy, even half asleep, even by my subconscious in a half-dream-world in which I was. I believe the author was the father of the girl whom I was to see the following day.

I definitely feel that it was the personality of her father, surviving so-called death, who gave me the instructions which explained in detail where a large sum of money was hidden in her home and of holdings in the Bahamas with explicit instructions to his daughter whom to contact, etc. All of this was subsequently verified.

The following day Anne visited me at the Church of Religious Science headquarters in New York City. I recognized her immediately, because I had seen her in my dream the night previously. There is a shining facet of our subconscious mind which reflects what is subjectively perceived and known, but which is not consciously known.

This girl was suffering from acute anxiety needlessly, because all the time her subconscious knew where the money was, and she could have communicated with it and received her answer. A knowledge of the laws of her mind has completely transformed the life of this girl, so that she is vital and alive and presently accomplishing great things.

Her Prayer Cast Out Her Fear

A young lady in New York City opened a music studio. She advertised extensively; weeks passed and not one student appeared on the scene. The reason for this was because the music teacher had the attitude of mind that she would fail and that students would not come to her because she was unknown. Her basic trouble was fear. She reversed her mental attitude and came to a decision that a great number of students could be benefited by what she had to offer. The following technique worked wonders in her professional career:

Twice daily she imagined herself teaching students and saw them happy and pleased. She was the actress in the drama, "Act as though I am, and I will be." She felt herself to be the successful teacher, acting the role in her imagination, and focusing her attention on her ideal. Through her persistence she became one with the idea in her mind until she succeeded in objectively expressing what she subjectively imagined and felt. She attracted more students than she could handle and eventually had to have an assistant.

What she imagined her life to be, she *felt* it to be, and according to her new feeling or mental attitude was it done unto her.

A Garden Gave Him Courage

During a series of lectures in 1958 in Capetown, South Africa, a brilliant lawyer listening to one of my lectures gave me a clipping dealing with forgiveness from a newspaper called *Argus*. The following is the essence of the article:

Lieutenant Colonel I. P. Carne told of his life as a prisoner in Korea. During his eighteen months in solitary confinement, he did not have a bitter word for the actions of his Chinese captors in imposing a sentence so harsh that doctors were amazed at his survival. In his imagination he walked around his garden (in England), and listened to the church bells welcoming him home. Lieutenant Colonel Carne said, "The mental picture of this glorious place (his loved ones, his garden, his home) forever kept my mind alive. Not for one moment did I let it slip away."

Instead of resenting and hating or indulging in mental recriminations, he gave himself a constructive vision. He imagined himself home with his loved ones; he felt the thrill and joy of it all. Visualizing the garden in full bloom, he saw the plants grow and bring forth fruit. It was vivid and real in his mind. He felt all this inwardly in his imagination. He said other men would have gone insane or perhaps would have died of a broken heart, but he saved himself because he had a vision. "It was a vision I never let slip away."

Lieutenant Colonel Carne's great secret was a new mental attitude in the midst of privation, misery, and squalor. He was loyal to his mental picture, and he never deviated from it by destructive inner talking or negative mental imagery. Finally, when he arrived home in England, he realized the significance of the profound truth that we go where our vision is.

He Cast Out His Unknown Fears

Following a recent series of lectures at the Science of Mind headquarters in San Francisco, a man visited me at my hotel. The first thing he said was, "I am haunted by unknown fears. I wake up at night perspiring copiously and shaking all over." He suffered frequently from acute paroxysmal attacks of asthma.

I found in talking to him that he had hated his father for many years because his father had bequeathed all his estate to his sister. This hatred developed a deep sense of guilt in his subconscious mind, and because of this guilt he had a deep, hidden fear of being punished; this complex expressed itself in his body as high blood pressure and asthmatic attacks.

Fear causes pain. Love and good will bring peace and health. The fear and guilt which this man had were expressed as disease, or lack of ease and peace.

This young man realized that his whole trouble was caused by his own sense of guilt, self-condemnation, and hatred. His father long since had passed to a higher dimension of life. Actually, the man was poisoning himself through hatred.

He began to forgive himself. *To forgive* is to give something for. He affirmed as follows, "I completely forgive my father. He did what he believed right according to his light. I release him. I wish him peace, harmony, and joy. I am sincere, and I mean it."

The young man lanced his psychic wound, and all the psychic pus came forth. His asthma disappeared, and his blood pressure dropped to normal. The fear of punishment which was lurking in his subconscious mind has now disappeared.

She Ceased Blocking the Answer

A woman wrote me saying, "I don't know what to do. I am full of fear. Shall I accept the new position offered me or stay where I am? Shall I keep or sell my home? Shall I marry the man with whom I am going? I must have answers right away; what decisions shall I make?"

Her fear of doing the wrong thing was blocking the answers to these perplexing questions. Furthermore, her fear was really based on ignorance and failure to understand the workings of her subconscious mind.

I explained to her that whenever her subconscious accepts an idea, immediately it begins to execute it. It uses all its mighty resources to that end and mobilizes all the unlimited mental and spiritual powers in our depths. This law is true for good or bad ideas.

The young lady ceased blocking her answer by such statements as, "I will never get an answer. I don't know what to do. I'm all mixed up." She came to a clear-cut conclusion in her conscious mind, knowing that Infinite Intelligence within her subconscious knows only the answer.

She prayed frequently as follows: "Infinite Intelligence is all-wise. The wisdom of my subconscious mind reveals to me the right answers. I am Divinely guided regarding my home and my selection of a husband, and I am confident Infinite Intelligence knows my hidden talents and guides me to my true place in life where I am doing what I love to do, Divinely happy and Divinely prospered."

This woman accepted a position in a legal office, married her employer, and both of them live in her home. There was a perfect solution and an ideal answer to all her requests. The wisdom of the subconscious is past finding out.

Wise Thoughts

If your thought is wise, the reaction or response will be wise. Your action is only the outer expression of your thought. Your constructive action or decision is but the manifestation of a wise or true thought entertained in your mind.

After asking for guidance or an answer to a particular problem, do not neglect obvious or convenient stepping stones to your goal. You will avoid blocking your answer when you simply think about the solution, knowing that your thought activates your subconscious, which knows all, sees all, and has the "know-how" of accomplishment.

Choose Confidence, Triumph, and Victory

The Bible says, "*Choose ye this day whom ye shall serve.*" The key to health, happiness, peace of mind, and abundance lies in the capacity *to choose*. When you learn to think right, you will cease choosing pain, misery, poverty, and limitation. On the contrary, you will choose from the treasure house of the Infinite within you. You will affirm incisively and decisively, "I choose happiness, peace, prosperity, wisdom, and security."

The moment you come to that definite conclusion in your conscious mind, your subconscious mind, full of the power and wisdom of the Infinite, will come to your aid. Guidance will come to you, and the way or path of achievement will be revealed to you.

Claim definitely and positively, without the slightest hesitation, doubt, or fear, "There is only one power of creation, and it is the power of my Deeper Self. There is a solution to every problem. This I know, decree, and believe." As you claim these truths boldly, you will receive guidance pertinent to all your undertakings, and wonders will happen in your life.

How He Overcame the Feeling of Frustration

To be frustrated is to be confused, baffled, perplexed, or thwarted in reaching your goal. Fear really is behind all frustration, because man believes he is stymied, blocked, and inhibited by external forces, and therefore he can't realize his desire. In other words, he thinks his environment is greater than himself.

A young engineer said to me some months ago, "I have been working for a boss for over fifteen years; I have not been promoted. My talents are being wasted. I'm so frustrated! I hate my boss—he is an ignoramous—and I just walked out and got another job. But I went from the frying pan into the fire. This new job is worse."

This engineer feared that he would never be advanced in his work because of his age and racial background. He was brought up by a domineering, tyrannical, puritanical sort of father who was typical of his New England traditions. He had resented his father and had not written him for several years. Moreover, he had a guilt' complex and feared punishment because of his hatred and resentment toward his father. He said to me, "I suppose God has it in for me."

Slowly but surely he began to see that he was rebelling against authority in the same way he had been rebelling inwardly against his father. It began to dawn on him that he was actually transferring the blame for his own shortcomings, mistakes, and misdeeds to his superiors in business. He was also attributing to those in authority over him his unacceptable impulses and thoughts.

He overcame his sense of frustration by first perceiving that he was actually blocking his own promotion by his fear, resentment, and hatred. He decided to pray morning and evening as follows: "I wish for everyone in the plant where I work health, happiness, peace, and promotion. My employer congratulates me on my work; I paint this picture in my mind regularly, and I know it will come to pass. I am loving, kind, and cooperative. I practice the golden rule, and I sincerely treat everyone in the same way that I would like to be treated. Divine Intelligence rules and guides me all day long, and I am prospered in all my ways."

As he saturated his mind regularly and systematically with these thoughts, he succeeded in bringing about a new mental attitude of a constructive nature which changed everything for the better in his life.

Five Positions in Five Months

I gave advice to a young man one time who was afraid of life, of the future, and of people. He was fearful that no matter what position he got, the boss and the other workers would not like him and he would be fired. He suffered from insomnia, alcoholism, and melancholia. He was also irresponsible, shiftless, lazy, crude, and lacking in zeal, understanding, and application.

I explained to him that his dominant attitude of fear colored everything and that his gloomy outlook caused him to look at life from the dark or negative side. The good news he received from his family from time to time brought about only an occasional mood of cheerfulness which was drowned out in a few minutes by his dominant gloomy and depressed attitude.

At my suggestion, this young man took a course in public speaking and another course at night school on the fundamentals of business where, with diligence, personal initiative, and application, he learned the rudiments of the commercial world. He began to pray for guidance and prosperity, claiming regularly that God was guiding him in all his ways and that he was prospered beyond his fondest dreams.

Gradually he commenced to die to the "old man" and "put on the new man." He developed enthusiasm, perseverance, stick-to-it-ive-ness, and eventually he became the foreman of the shop where he worked. He became happy and joyous and began to express health, harmony, and true living.

This man learned that practically all teaching, whether institutional, religious, or secular, has for its real purpose the inducement of a changed mental attitude toward life, people, and events. The first step in banishing his abnormal fear and in his onward march was correcting his attitude towards life.

How to Realize Your Desire

No man can serve two masters. A man cannot expect to realize the desire of his heart if he believes there is a power which thwarts that desire. This creates a conflict, and his mind is divided. He stands still and he gets nowhere. His mind must move as a unity. Infinity cannot be divided or multiplied. The Infinite must be one— a unity. There cannot be two Infinities, as one would quarrel with the other; they would neutralize or cancel out each other. We would have a chaos instead of a cosmos. Unity of the spirit is a mathematical necessity, for there is no opposition to the one Power. If there were some power to challenge God, or the Infinite One, God would cease to be Omnipotent or Supreme.

You can see what confusion and chaos reign in the minds of people who believe in two opposing powers. Their minds are divided because they have two masters, and this belief creates a conflict, causing their power and strength to be divided. Learn to go in one direction only by believing that God who gave you the desire will also show you how to fulfill it.

Take a Personal Inventory

Are you experiencing friction, misunderstanding, and resentment in your relationships with others? These unsatisfactory personal adjustments are due to the bad company you are keeping in your mind. When you were young, your mother warned you to keep away from bad company, and if you disobeyed you were soundly spanked. In a somewhat similar manner, you must not walk down the dark alleys of your mind and keep the company of resentment, fear, worry, ill will, and hostility; these are the thieves of your mind which rob you of poise, balance, harmony, and health.

You must positively and definitely refuse to walk and talk with them in the galleries of your mind. On the contrary, you must make it a practice to walk the sunlit streets of your mind, associating with lovely, spiritual companions called confidence, peace, faith, love, joy, good will, health, happiness, guidance, inspiration, and abundance. You can choose your companions in the objective world, and I feel sure that when you do you will select them according to the criteria of honesty and integrity.

You select your clothes, work, friends, teachers, books, home, and food. You are a choosing, volitional being. When you choose something, you portray a preference for one thing over another; it may be a hat or a pair of shoes. Having taken a personal inventory of the contents of your mind, choose health, happiness, peace, and abundance, and you will reap fabulous dividends.

Understanding Banishes Needless Suffering

You must give up your false beliefs, opinions, and theories and exchange them for the truth which sets you free. You are not a ictim of your five senses; neither are you controlled by external conditions or environment. You can change conditions by changing your mental attitude. Your thought and feeling create your destiny and determine your experience. Therefore, you can no longer blame others for your misery, pain, or failure.

When you see clearly that what you think, feel, believe, and give mental consent to, consciously or unconsciously, determines all happenings, events, and circumstances of your life, you will cease to fear, resent, condemn, and blame others. You will discover there is no one to change but yourself.

You Create Your Own Heaven

For countless centuries, man has looked outside himself and filled his mind with jealousies, hates, fears, resentment, and depression, due to his belief that others were marring his happiness and causing his troubles. He has believed that he is the victim of fate, chance, and accidents, and that there are other powers and forces inimical to his welfare. His mind is full of all sorts of weird ideas, superstitions, anxieties, and complicated philosophies about devils, evil entities, and malevolent forces.

The truth is that man's thought is creative; his habitual thinking becomes his abundance or his poverty. Man must divest himself of all his erroneous and false concepts and realize that he makes his own heaven (harmony and peace) and his own hell (misery and suffering) here and now.

A man can influence his subconscious positively or negatively. The subconscious mind is always amoral and impersonal, and it has no ethics or sentiments. Hence, if man's thoughts are of an evil nature, the law of the subconscious mind will automatically bring these thoughts into form and experience. If man's thoughts are good, wholesome, and constructive, the law of his subconscious will bring forth good experiences and happy circumstances.

This is neither more nor less than the law of cause and effect, which is a universal and impersonal law.

Retribution and Reward

Your retribution and reward depend on how you use your mind. If you make an erroneous decision in your mind, you invoke the mathematical and just response of the law of your subconscious mind, and you will experience loss as a result of your erroneous judgment or decision. The law of action and reaction is universal throughout nature. If your thoughts are wise, your actions will be wise.

God is not vengeful or vindictive, but the impersonal law of your own mind reacts and responds according to what is impressed upon it. Your thought-life produces what seems to look like vengeance when you are unawakened to the way your mind works. Actually, you are experiencing a natural law of action and reaction which is always equal, exact, and precise. There would be no point in blaming the lake if your friend should happen to fall in and be drowned when he lacks the ability to swim. You would not accuse the lake of vengeance; the water is completely impersonal.

> *I sent my soul through the Invisible*
> *Some letter of that after-life to spell,*
> *And by and by my soul returned to me*
> *And answered, "I myself am Heaven and Hell."*
> Omar Khayyam

The Secret Place

I suggest you quiet the wheels of your mind frequently and dwell on these great eternal truths which live in the hearts of all men. As you affirm the following prayer regularly, systematically, and joyously, you will feel rejuvenated, revitalized, and energized spiritually, mentally, and physically:

> *"He that dwelleth in the secret place of the most High shall abide under the shadow of the Almighty."*
> I dwell in the secret place of the most High; this is my own mind. All the thoughts entertained by me conform to harmony, peace, and good will. My mind is the

dwelling place of happiness, joy, and a deep sense of security. All the thoughts that enter my mind contribute to my joy, peace, and general welfare. I live, move, and have my being in the atmosphere of good fellowship, love, and unity.

All the people that dwell in my mind are God's children. I am at peace in my mind with all the members of my household and all mankind. The same good I wish for myself, I wish for all men. I am living in the house of God now. I claim peace and happiness, for I know I dwell in the house of the Lord forever.

IMPORTANT POINTERS

1. Eradicate fear by joining mentally and emotionally with the God-Presence within you.
2. If you can't find something, ask your subconscious and it will reveal the answer to you.
3. Many times hatred is the cause of fear of being punished. Forgive the other and go free.
4. Fear of failure will attract failure. Expect success, and good fortune will smile on you.
5. If confined or restricted, get a mental vision and mentally adhere to it. Be loyal to it, and you will go where your vision is.
6. Fear is behind many physical ailments. Fill your mind with love and good will, and you will be free.
7. Never say, "I am full of fear," or "I am all mixed up." Your subconscious takes these statements literally, and you remain confused.
8. If your thoughts are wise, your actions will be wise.
9. The key to health, happiness, and peace of mind lies in the capacity to choose the abundant life.
10. You don't have to be frustrated. Realize God who gave you the desire will bring it to pass in Divine order. There is no power to oppose Omnipotence.
11. A changed attitude changes everything. Become enthusiastic, believe in yourself and in your hidden powers, and wonders will happen in your life.
12. The double-minded man is unstable in all his ways.

Be single-minded. Recognize the One Power, and then your mind will move as a unity.

13. The cause of all the trouble in your life is due to the kind of company you are keeping in your mind. Take inventory now.

14. Your thought and feeling create your destiny. There is no one to blame but yourself.

15. Man creates his own hell and his own heaven here and now by the way he thinks all day long.

16. Retribution or reward depends on how you use your mind. The law of action and reaction is universal throughout nature. Think good, good follows. Think evil, evil follows.

The
𝔚onderful 𝔏aw
of security

The feeling of security or of insecurity is due primarily to your basic approach to life. A distinguished research physician, associated with the University of California in Los Angeles, told me the other day that he has never found a patient with a strong sense of security who suffers from chronic worry, fear complexes, or mental disorders of any kind. The doctor attributed this sense of security to an abiding faith and trust in a Supreme Power which watches over man in all his ways.

If you have not learned about your own essential greatness and the infinite riches within you, you tend to magnify the problems and the difficulties which confront you, imparting to them powers and magnitude which you fail to attribute to yourself.

One of the main reasons for your feeling of insecurity is that you are making the externals of life *causes,* not realizing that they are *effects.*

How to Get the Feeling of Security

The first thing you have to realize is that there is no real security apart from your sense of oneness with God—the Source of all blessings. By applying the principles described in this book, you can develop a practical, workable, sane, and marvelous feeling of inner security. There is an urge within each of us that cries out for union with an Eternal Source. Join up now with this Infinite Power, and you will immediately draw upon Its strength.

You are immersed in an infinite ocean of Life—the Infinite Mind—which constantly permeates you entirely and in which you live, move, and *have* your being. Remember that this Infinite Power has never been defeated or frustrated by anything outside Itself. This Infinite Power is omnipotent, and when you consciously unite with It through your thought and feeling, you immediately become greater than that which you feared.

The Infinite lies stretched in smiling repose within you—this is the true state of your mind. The power and wisdom of this Infinite Mind become potent and active in your life the moment you recognize Its existence and establish your mental contact with It. If you do this now, you will experience immediately a marvelous feeling of inner security, and you will discover the peace that passeth understanding.

He Stopped Praying Against Himself

I should like to cite the following case: A friend of mine was involved in a long-delayed lawsuit which had cost him a considerable sum of money in legal fees. His attorney had told him that he would probably lose the case, and this meant that he would be more or less penniless. He was terrified and, while discussing the matter with me, said that there was nothing left to live for and that the only thing to do was to *end it all.*

I explained to him that these utterances were highly destructive and undoubtedly played a major role in prolonging the case. Every time this man expressed these negative words, in actual fact he had been praying against himself.

I asked him a simple question: "What would you say if I told you this minute that there had been a perfect, harmonious solution and the whole matter was concluded?"

He replied, "I would be delighted and eternally grateful! I would feel wonderful, knowing that the whole thing was finished."

My friend then agreed to see to it that his inner, silent thought would conform to his desired aim, which was a successful conclusion of the legal case. Regularly and systematically, he applied the following prayer which I gave to him: "I give thanks for the perfect, harmonious solution which takes place through the wisdom of the All-Wise One."

He frequently repeated this prayer to himself during the day, and when difficulties, delays, set-backs, arguments, doubts, and fear came to his mind, he would silently affirm the above truth. He completely ceased making negative statements, and he also controlled his silent thoughts, knowing that his inner thought and feeling always would be made manifest.

It is what you feel on the inside that is made manifest. You can say one thing with your mouth and feel another way in your heart; it is what you feel on the inside that is reproduced on the screen of space.

This man learned through practice and discipline never to affirm inwardly anything he did not want to experience outwardly. His lips and his heart agreed on a harmonious solution to his legal case, and Divine Justice prevailed. Additional information was provided from a completely unexpected source, and the lawsuit was resolved so that he did not suffer a financial loss.

My friend had realized that his security was dependent upon his alignment with the Infinite Presence, which moved as unity, harmony, justice, and right action, and he discovered that nothing could oppose the Infinite Power which moves the world.

The End of My Rope

Recently a young man said to me, "I'm at the end of my rope. I have a blood disorder which is incurable." He was full of anxiety, fear, and doubt. His relatives repeatedly reminded him that his healing would take a long time and that he might never be cured. Fortunately, his wise doctor encouraged him and advised him to stay away from his relatives.

I explained to him that his subconscious mind was receiving all the negative statements about himself made by his relatives and that as long as he persisted in listening to them, he could not experience a healing. He was insecure because he did not know that the Infinite Healing Presence which created his body could heal Its own handiwork.

This young man began to talk in a different tone to his subconscious mind. As he listened carefully and avidly, I told him to affirm slowly, quietly, lovingly, and feelingly, the following prayer:

> The Creative Intelligence which made my body is now re-creating my blood. The Healing Presence knows how to heal, and It is transforming every cell of my body to God's perfect pattern. I hear and see the doctor telling me that I am whole. I have this picture now in my mind. I see him clearly and I hear his voice; he is saying to me, "John, you are healed! It is a miracle!" I know that this constructive imagery is going down deep into my subcon-

scious mind, where it is being developed and brought to pass. I know that the Infinite Healing Presence is now restoring me in spite of all sensory evidence to the contrary. I feel this, I believe it, and I am now identifying with my aim—perfect health.

He repeated this prayer four or five times daily for ten or fifteen minutes, particularly prior to falling asleep at night. Due to his old habits, he found his mind running wild at times, and he found himself fretting, fussing, worrying, and recounting the verdict of others and his repeated failings in the healing process. When these thoughts came to his mind, he learned to issue the order, "Stop! I am the master over all of my thoughts, imagery, and responses, and they must obey me. From now on, all of my thoughts are on God and His healing power. This is the way I feed my subconscious; I constantly identify with God, and my inner thought and feeling is 'Thank you, Father!' I do this a hundred times a day, or a thousand times, if necessary."

This young man had a healing of his blood condition in three months. By repetition, prayer, and meditation, he established new habits of positive thought, and he succeeded in aligning his subconscious mind with his desire. He proved the truth in the Bible, "*Thy faith hath made thee whole.*" (Matthew 9:22)

Your security is not determined by your stocks, bonds, real estate, or other investments. Security depends upon your inner *feeling* of security, which is your sense of faith and trust in the ever-availability of God's love and supply meeting all your needs at every moment of time and point of space.

Security Cannot Be Legislated

No government—no matter how well-intentioned it might be— can guarantee you peace, happiness, joy, abundance, or security. You cannot determine exactly all of the events, circumstances, and experiences through which you will pass on your life's journey. Unforeseen cataclysms, floods, earthquakes, typhoons, and monsoons will take place, which may destroy cities and properties and wipe out the holdings of thousands of people. Wars, insurrections, and political upheavals take place from time to time, which have unpredictable effects on currency and real estate. International tragedies and fear of war have had catastrophic effects on the stock markets of the world.

All material possessions are vulnerable to change, and there actually is no real security in stocks, bonds, or money in the bank. For example, the value of a ten-dollar bill depends on the integrity and honesty of our government and its ability to back up a sound currency. A check from a bank or from another person really is only a piece of paper, and its value depends on the honesty and integrity of the writer of the check and on your faith in the soundness of the bank.

Pray and Protect Your Investments

If you devote some time and attention every day to scientific prayer and meditation, you will experience a changed mental attitude, and you cannot and will not suffer from the many hazards and unforeseen catastrophes which are enumerated in this chapter.

Walk in the consciousness of God's eternal supply. Know in your heart that the Overshadowing Presence is watching over you in all your ways. Remember that as long as you maintain a prosperity consciousness you cannot suffer losses. For example, if your oil well suddenly dried up and this happened to be the channel through which your money comes to you, as much money as you need automatically would come to you from some other source. The amount you would receive definitely would be equal to the income you had previously derived from the oil well.

When you build into your mentality the awareness of the Eternal Source of supply, you cannot become impoverished, and no matter what form wealth takes you always will be amply supplied.

Prayer Controlled His Ups and Downs

I talked with a man a few weeks ago who complained bitterly about his ups and downs. He said, "Sometimes I make a small fortune in the stock market, and shortly afterward I experience a great loss. At times, I enjoy robust health, but periodically I find myself in the hospital for various ailments. Fortune and misfortune are my lot. Can't something be done to stop these great swings of fate?"

I explained to this man that it is possible to maintain a constant upbeat and to lead a balanced life in which serenity and tranquility reign supreme. It is true that most people swing from exhilaration one day to a mood of depression the next day when something goes wrong. Many people constantly are going from "black Monday" to "bright Tuesday."

This man realized that life would be very insipid, dull, and monotonous without any variations, challenges, or problems. Tragedies, emergencies, and exigencies come into the lives of nearly all people. It is possible to regulate our emotional reactions so that neither the upbeat nor the downbeat is overly accentuated.

The first step this man had to take was to purposefully acquire mental and emotional control. He soon realized that he could preserve his equanimity regardless of circumstances. While speaking about man's vicissitudes and misfortunes, Marcus Aurelius said, "Nothing happens to any man which he is not formed by nature to bear." In Hawaii a guide will show you a hut where the great writer, Robert Louis Stevenson, wrote a masterpiece, *Treasure Island,* despite the fact that he was suffering from an acute case of tuberculosis!

I gave my friend a spiritual prescription to follow, whereby he would find strength and assurance from the kingdom of God within him. He prayed frequently during each day, dwelling on these eternal verities:

> "*Thou wilt keep him in perfect peace, whose mind is stayed on thee: because he trusteth in thee.*" (Isaiah 26:3) I know that the inner desires of my heart come from God within me. God wants me to be happy. God's will for me is life, love, truth, and beauty. I mentally accept my good now, and I become a perfect channel for the Divine. I am an expression of God. I am Divinely directed in all my ways, and I am always in my true place, doing the thing I love to do. I refuse to accept as truth the opinions of man, for my mind is a part of God's mind, and I am always reflecting Divine wisdom and Divine intelligence. God's ideas unfold within my mind in perfect sequence. I am always poised, balanced, serene, and calm, for I know that God always will reveal to me the perfect solution to all my needs. The Lord is my shepherd; I shall not want for any good thing. I am Divinely active and Divinely creative. I sense and feel the rhythm of God. I hear the melody of God whispering its message of love to me.

A completely balanced life followed after he had made himself a part of God's fulfillment by thinking in the above manner.

How She Healed Her Sense of Loss

A young woman said to me at a recent funeral service, "My father changed his will and left everything to my brother. I have lost everything. My heart was set on receiving half of the estate."

This young lady felt a deep sense of loss, and she feared the future. Fear always can be replaced by faith in God and all things good, once we know how to use our mind. In talking to her, I explained that she could never really lose anything unless she accepted the loss in her mind, as all experiences take place through the mind.

Let us say that I have "lost" my watch. This really means that it is somewhere, but I can't find it just now. I know that it might have fallen on the street, or perhaps I left it in a phone booth, or it might be that a pickpocket has it. Whatever has happened to it, the watch is not lost in the Infinite Mind of God. "Nothing is lost in all my Holy Mountain." Infinite Mind permeates and indwells every particle of matter in the universe. The watch is an idea in Mind, and even though my watch may have been destroyed, the mind of man can create millions of watches. In other words, God can't lose anything.

She decided to heal her fear of loss and her deep sense of insecurity, which had caused her so much mental anguish. Her first step was to acquire an understanding of a law of mind, which is that no one can rob us of our good without our mental consent, by fearing or believing in loss. The second step was to make a definite mental *choice*, knowing that her choice of God's riches and wealth, when given attention and steadily adhered to, would be accepted by her subconscious mind and brought to pass in her experience. Her third step was to remain faithful to the idea that God's wealth was flowing into her experience, knowing in her heart that her belief in God's promises would result in fulfillment. This attitude of mind rapidly dissolved her sense of loss. Her mind began to move with God's mind—in one direction. How incongruous and ludicrous it would be to assume that the Infinite Mind of God could move in two directions!

The following prayer became her fourth step:

"In quietness and in confidence shall be your strength."
(Isaiah 30:15) I know that my inner feeling of security
is based on my knowledge that God takes care of me, and
I have confidence in His direction. My greatest security
is that I know and feel God's Presence. I know deep
down in my heart that God is the Source of all life and
all blessings. God is with me and for me, He watches
over me, He cares for me, He provides for me, He sup-
ports me, and He loves me. My thoughts are thoughts
of fulfillment, since all of God's desires always are being
fulfilled. He restoreth my soul and my thought life. His
goodness and mercy follow me all the days of my life,
for I have *chosen* to dwell mentally and spiritually with
God all the days of my life.

A month after having prayed in the above manner, she was
asked to attend a political reception in Los Angeles, at which
she met a very prominent physician. Two months later, they were
married. This physician said to her that she was the only spiritually minded woman he had met, and he was deeply impressed
by her poise, self-assurance, and inner sense of tranquillity. Her
belief in the fulfillment of her prayer brought results.

Life is always eminently fair. The ups and downs, sickness,
turmoil, strife, and misfortune that at times beset our existence
are the consequences of our misuse of the laws of mind and the
results of our false and superstitious beliefs.

Building a Glorious Future

Go to work in your thoughts, tune in on the Infinite One, and
affirm boldly, "I am compassed about with songs of deliverance."
Almightly God is within you. You are equipped to lead a
glorious and wonderful life, for all the power of God is available

to you. You should release His wisdom, power, and glory in your life.

If you don't use your muscles, they will inevitably atrophy. You have mental and spiritual "muscles" which must be exercised, also. If your thoughts, attitudes, motivations, and reactions are not God-like, your contact with God is broken, and you become depressed, rejected, fearful, morose, and morbid.

Look *within.* "*The kingdom of God is within you.*" God's power, wisdom, and strength to meet any and all challenges is within you. In the Book of Daniel (Ch. 11 v. 32), you will read, "*The people that do know their God shall be strong, and do exploits.*"

> "*Behold, I am the Lord, the God of all flesh:*
> *Is there any thing too hard for me?*"
> Jeremiah 32:27

A HEALTHY REVIEW

1. Your worries and fears really are due to your failure to align yourself with the Infinite, which knows no fear or opposition.
2. No real security can take place apart from your feeling of oneness with God.
3. Your inner, silent thought must agree with your aims in life; otherwise, your prayer can't be answered.
4. When you are constantly mentally denying what you are affirming outwardly, you cannot get a healing.
5. A real sense of security is not dependent upon bonds, stocks, and real estate. The real feeling of security is based on faith and trust in God—the Giver of all gifts.
6. A government cannot guarantee security, peace, or happiness. You decree your own security, peace, joy, and health through the laws of your mind.
7. You protect your investments by knowing that all your possessions are watched over by the Overshadowing Presence, and you dwell constantly in the *Secret Place.*
8. Avoid ups and downs by realizing that Divine law and order govern your life, and that God thinks, speaks, acts, and directs all your undertakings. Make a habit of this prayer, and poise and balance will be yours.
9. Fear can be replaced by faith in God and His eternal

supply. *"In quietness and in confidence lie your strength."*

10. You can lead a glorious and wonderful life by joining up with God and by knowing that God's power, wisdom, and strength are there to meet all problems. When you begin, God begins. *"I and my Father are One."*

The
𝕸*agical* 𝕷*aw*
of mental nutrition

I have
known people who have had the choicest food and a perfectly
balanced diet, according to the laws of nutrition, and yet they
developed ulcers, cancer, arthritis, and other destructive and
degenerative diseases.

The food of your experiences, conditions, and events is your
thought life. Your habitual thinking nourishes and sustains
your conditions and causes them to increase and magnify in your
experience. Fear thoughts, worry and critical thoughts, and
angry and hateful thoughts are the food of sickness, despond-
ence, failure, and misery.

All of us know that all living creatures follow their food.
Explorers and scientists tell us that animal life is absent in parts

of the globe where food is unobtainable. All kinds of life abound where food is plentiful. When you feed your mind with all kinds of negative food, all sorts of sickness, lack, misery, and suffering come into your life—because they seek their food.

You Are What You Mentally Eat

All of us have heard the expression, "You are what you eat." If a thing is true, there is a way in which it is true. You are what you eat psychologically and spiritually. Thoughts of God, thoughts of love, kindness, optimism, joy, and good will, are the foods of health, joy, happiness, and success; if you mentally absorb and digest a bountiful supply of these foods, you will attract and experience all these things in your life.

If you are hateful, envious, jealous, and full of hostility, the physical food you eat may well be transformed into various diseases of a psychosomatic nature. Contrariwise, if you are full of good will and eat the food on the table with joy and thanksgiving, it will be transmuted into beauty, vitality, wholesomeness, and strength. The bread or meat which you eat, becomes your flesh and blood after a few hours. This is essentially the meaning of "you are what you eat."

The Importance of Diet

Food for the body is very important. Today some of our foremost research physicians are pointing out the dangers of excessive fat, which interferes with the mechanical efficiency of all our vital organs such as the heart, lungs, liver, and kidneys. We know that many physical and mental diseases can result from lack of certain vitamins and chemicals. Beriberi, a disease characterized by multiple inflammatory changes in the nerves, producing great muscular debility, is brought about by an insufficiency of vitamin B. We are all familiar with the necessity of sufficient calcium for the pregnant mother. Deficiency of vitamin A has deleterious effects on the eyes, and a sufficient amount of protein is essential for our well-being.

All this is most important, but our mental and spiritual diet also is of the greatest importance.

The Bread of Love and Peace

I knew a man who wrote a wonderful book on nutrition. It was quite scientific and very sound; however, he had acute ulcers and was most unhappy. His physician prescribed a simple diet which he had been on for eight months, with little or no improvement. This was due to the fact that when he read the newspapers or listened to the radio and press reports, headlining suffering, crime, injustice, and man's inhumanity to man, he would get furious and write poison-pen letters to congressmen and others, pouring out his vituperation and telling them what he thought of them. Furthermore, the vexation, strife, and contention during the business day unduly upset him.

This man changed his mental and emotional diet. The mental regimen was as follows: "I am going to transform all negative impressions that come to me during the day. From now on, I will never permit news, propaganda, criticism, or negative statements of others to promote negative reactions in me. When I am tempted to react negatively and vindictively, I will stop immediately and affirm to myself boldly, 'God thinks, speaks, and acts through me now. His river of peace floods my mind and heart, and I am identified with my aim, which is peace and harmony.'"

By making a habit of reacting this way, he was eating the

bread of love and peace, and in a short period of time he had a remarkable healing.

Your Mental and Spiritual Diet

The Bible says "Thou shalt not eat any abominable thing," which means that you should not entertain or enthrone in your mind negative thoughts such as resentment, ill will, cynicism, hate, or anger.

Distinguished research physicians and other scientists point out that we have a new body every eleven months. You are creating new cells all the time, and if you fill your mind with the eternal verities and spiritual values of life, your brain will send these spiritual vibrations through the medium of your nervous system all over your body, and all the new cells will take on the vibrations of these spiritual overtones, so that like Job you will be able to say: "*Yet in my flesh shall I see God.*"

You need a special mental and spiritual diet. You are fed daily through the five senses by an avalanche of sights, sounds, and sundry concepts—good and bad—but most of this food is highly unsavory. You must learn to turn inward to God and be replenished from the standpoint of Truth. For example, affirm frequently with feeling: "God is guiding me now. God's love fills my soul, God inspires me, and God illumines my pathway in life. I radiate love and good will to all. Divine law and order govern my life at all times."

This prayer is a wonderful spiritual diet for your mind. Wonders will happen as you make a habit of this prayer.

His Head Knowledge Became Heart Knowledge

A man in San Francisco said to me, "I have read all the books on mental healing, and I have written several articles myself on the use of the healing power of the subconscious, but I have not been able to heal myself of a chronic condition—colitis."

In talking with him, I discovered that he failed to meditate, reflect, and mentally digest what he read and wrote about the healing powers of the subconscious mind so that it would be incorporated into his subconscious mind.

He had studied the various religions of the world, had read a vast number of inspirational books, had studied numerology and astrology, and seemed to be a charter member of every new and strange cult. He was so muddled, perplexed, and confused that actually he was mentally and emotionally disoriented and unbalanced.

I outlined a simple plan for him by suggesting that he select what is eternally true, and that all his reading, thought-life, instruction, and decisions must meet and conform to the following standard: ". . . *Whatsoever things are true, whatsoever things are honest, whatsoever things are just, whatsoever things are pure, whatsoever things are lovely, whatsoever things are of good report; if there be any virtue, and if there be any praise, think on these things.*" Phil. 4:8.

He accepted this spiritual standard which enabled him to choose what is noble and God-like for the sanctuary of his own mind. Anything and everything that did not conform to this spiritual standard was positively and definitely rejected as unfit for the house of God, his own mind. He meditated on the following prayer five or six times daily:

> "*He that dwelleth in the secret place of the most High shall abide under the shadow of the Almighty.*" I dwell in the secret place of the most High; this is my own mind. All the thoughts entertained by me conform to harmony, peace, and good will. My mind is the dwelling place of happiness, joy, and a deep sense of security. All the thoughts that enter my mind contribute to my joy, peace, and general welfare. I live, move, and have my

being in the atmosphere of good fellowship, love, and unity.

All the people that dwell in my mind are God's children. I am at peace in my mind with all the members of my household and all mankind. The same good I wish for myself, I wish for all men. I am living in the house of God now. I claim peace and happiness, for I know I dwell in the house of the Lord forever.

Gradually, his head knowledge of God's ideas became heart knowledge, and his chronic colitis was no more.

His Mental Imagery Healed Him

I knew a man in New York City who would never leave his home. He would not go out into the street or even into his yard. Whenever he planned to leave his home, he would imagine all the dire things that could happen to him. He would feel faint and dizzy. This condition is called "agoraphobia." The fear originated in his early childhood due to the fact that when he was about five years old, he wandered away from home and was lost in the woods for several hours. His memory of being lost and the anxiety ensuing from it were lurking in his subconscious mind.

He freed himself by using his imagination correctly. At my suggestion, he began to spend about ten minutes, three times a day, imagining he was riding in a streetcar, peacefully reading, or that he was visiting stores, entering the library, buying groceries, or calling on friends. He began to feel the reality of all this.

Gradually, these constructive images penetrated the deeper layers of his subconscious mind and expunged from his deeper mind the fear pattern lodged there for several years. What he imagined and felt as true came to pass.

The Thankful Heart

Use the following prayer frequently, and you will find yourself close to God, and all the food that you eat will be transmuted into beauty.

> I give supreme recognition to the God-Presence within me. I sincerely and honestly give thanks for all the blessings received. I give thanks for all the good in my life; I live in the feeling of grateful rejoicing. My thankful heart strikes the magic of the Divine response. Every day of my life I express thanks for my knowledge of the laws of mind and the way of the Spirit. I know that thankfulness is a movement of the heart first, which is followed by a movement of the lips. My uplifted heart opens up the treasure-house of Infinity within me and bespeaks my faith in the fulfillment of my prayers. I am truly thankful because I have found God in the midst of me. *"I sought the Lord, and He heard me and delivered me from all my fears."* He who possesses a thankful heart is always in tune with the Infinite and cannot suppress the joy that arises from contemplating God and His Holy Presence. In everything, I give thanks.

HIGHLIGHTS TO RECALL

1. The food of your experiences, conditions, and events is your thought-life.
2. All living creatures follow their food. Sickness, misery, pain, and suffering follow negative mental attitudes, because they seek their food.
3. You are what you eat psychologically and spiritually. Eat your food with joy and thanksgiving.
4. Food for the body is important, but our mental and spiritual diet is of supreme importance.
5. You can mentally transform all negative impressions that come to you through your five senses. Start now!
6. You have a new body every eleven months. Fill your mind with the eternal verities and you will become rejuvenated and revitalized.
7. Intellectual assent is not enough. The truths you accept consciously must be emotionalized and felt as true, thereby assimilated by the subconscious mind.
8. Your head knowledge must be incorporated into your subconscious mind (the heart); then your head knowledge will become heart knowledge, and your prayers will be answered.
9. You take a vacation from fear when you focus your attention on whatsoever things are true, noble, lofty, and God-like. When fear thoughts knock at the door of your mind, let faith in God open the door, and there is no one there.
10. Fear is based on distorted, twisted imagination. Im-

agine you are doing the thing you are afraid to do, and the death of fear is certain.

11. The thankful heart is always close to God. Be thankful, and bless His Name.

The
𝕲reat 𝕷aw
of love

If you
want to remain healthy, vigorous, and strong, you have to realize
that there is but one Power, indivisible, and Its source is love.
This Power has no opposition. It is the omnipotent Life Principle that has overcome every opposition in this world and It
goes on conquering and is forever victorious. Realize that you
are one with this God-Power. You are aligned with It now, and
mighty forces will come to your aid.

Love Is Always Outgoing

Love must have an object. Love is an emotional attachment.
You can fall in love with music, art, a great project, a cause, or

with your ideal. You can become emotionally attracted to the eternal verities. You can become absorbed and engrossed in science and many other things.

Einstein loved the principle of mathematics, and it revealed its secrets to him. That is what love does. Astronomers fall in love with the science of astronomy, and they are constantly revealing the secrets of the heavens to us.

How Much Do You Want to Be a New Person?

Do you want to leave your old self—with your false concepts and old-fashioned ideas? Are you willing to get new ideas, new imagery, new viewpoints? Are you open and receptive? If you are, you must give up your resentments, grudges, peeves, fears, jealousies, and hates. If you wish to go from Los Angeles to New York, you must first leave Los Angeles. Likewise, if you want to be a new person, you must give up your fears and hates and you must focus your attention on the concepts of harmony, health, peace, joy, love, and good will in order to enter into the joy of living.

Why the Actor Failed Three Times

An actor said to me, "I am going to fail. I am going to strike the wrong note. I am going to say the wrong thing."

His vivid imagination was centered on failure. He had to fall in love with a new concept of himself to become the great artist that he now is. He became emotionally attached and absorbed with a new estimate, a new blueprint of himself.

His Prayer of Triumph

At my suggestion he isolated himself in his room three or four times a day where he was not disturbed, settling himself comfortably in his armchair, and relaxing his body to the utmost. This physical inertia rendered his mind more receptive to his affirmations. He affirmed for about five minutes at each sitting as follows: "I am completely relaxed and at ease. I am poised, serene, and calm. At the audition I sing beautifully, majestically, and gloriously. The auditor congratulates me. I am at peace in my mind."

He had a number of such "sittings" every day for about a week, and particularly at night prior to sleep. Having carried out this plan with assurance and conviction, he succeeded admirably and he is now a wonderful actor acclaimed by thousands.

Love of God and What It Means

The words *God* and *good* are synonymous. When you mentally and emotionally unite with honesty, integrity, justice, good will, and happiness, you are loving God, because you are loving that which is good. You are loving God when you are fascinated, absorbed, and captivated by the great truth that God is One and Indivisible and there are no divisions or quarrels in It. To love God is to give your allegiance, loyalty, and devotion to the One Power, refusing to recognize any other power in the world. When you definitely recognize and completely accept in your mind that God really is omnipotent, in the most practical, literal, and matter-of-fact manner, you are loving God, because you are loyal to the One Power. Sit down quietly at times and think over this vital, interesting, fascinating, and greatest of all truths that God is the only Power and that everything we can be aware of is part of His self-expression.

Love and Fear Cannot Dwell Together

An actress said to me at Caxton Hall, London, England, where I was giving a series of lectures on *The Power of Your Subconscious Mind*, "I heard you say love and fear can't dwell together. I am full of fear, and that's why I don't get better parts."

I told her to fall in love with a nobler, sweeter, grander concept of herself. She came to a decision to fall in love with her Greater Self—the God-Presence within her. She began to dwell on the fact that she possessed almost illimitable possibilities of development and that there *were* powers within her that had never been released. She began to affirm regularly and systematically: "I can do all things through the God-Power which flows through me. God thinks, speaks, and acts through me, and I am a wonderful and successful actress. The Infinite is always successful, and I am one with the Infinite. I am a child of God, and what is true of Him is true of me." When fear and worry thoughts came into her mind, she would affirm, "God's love fills my soul," or, "God is with me now." After a few weeks, all the sense of fear and insecurity passed away.

She has had many promotions and financial recognition in her particular field since that time. God's power captivated her imagination. It thrilled her through and through, and she became entranced with the idea of being a great actress. This love caused her to unite with her ideal. She did not try to hold the ideal; the ideal captivated her. That is love; then all fear went away. Fear was swallowed up in love, because love and fear cannot dwell together.

Love Conquers Jealousy

Shakespeare said, "Oh, beware of jealousy; it is the green-eyed monster, which doth mock the meat it feeds on." Milton said, "Jealousy is the injured lover's hell." Actually, the jealous man poisons his own banquet and then eats it. Jealousy is a mental poison, and the cause of it is fear. The jealous person demands exclusive devotion and is intolerant of rivalry. Furthermore, the jealous person is suspiciously watchful regarding the fidelity of husband, wife, lover, or friend. Basically, jealousy arises from a deep-seated fear or mistrust of another plus a feeling of guilt and uncertainty about oneself.

One husband said to me that his wife was abnormally jealous. She was constantly accusing him of having other women. She insisted there was a rival of whom she was unaware. He added that his wife practiced with the Ouija board which told her that he was unfaithful.

In talking to his wife at her husband's request, I explained to her in detail that it was her own subconscious mind which was confirming her suspicion and resentment toward her husband. She began to see clearly that it was her deeper mind that, through imperceptible movements of her fingers, operated the Ouija board. In other words, she was simply talking to herself. While talking with the husband I had found out that he was depleted and was taking a series of treatments from a physician. The woman was honest enough to see her error, and both of them agreed to send forth thoughts of love, peace, and kindliness to one another. This good will dissolved the negative attitudes and brought peace where discord and suspicion had reigned. The explanation was the cure. This woman learned to trust her husband, and where love and trust exist, there is no jealousy.

The Lord Giveth the Increase

The scientific thinker substitutes the word "Law" for "Lord" in the Bible. This is the law of your subconscious mind which magnifies whatever you deposit in it. It is an impersonal law of cause and effect.

I explained to a local real estate operator the meaning of "the Lord giveth the increase." He had not made a sale in four months. The reason was that he was giving attention to the negatives, such as poor business, no sale, financial loss, and inability to pay bills. Gradually his condition got very much worse, and he suffered from loss of prestige, health, finances, sickness in his family, and, finally, no business at all.

He discovered it was far more interesting, fascinating, alluring, and captivating to contemplate success, harmony, wealth, peace of mind, more satisfied customers, and better service to his clients. I gave him the following prayer, which I suggested he repeat out loud, slowly, quietly, and lovingly, five or six times a day until he reconditioned his mind to success and wealth:

> I believe in my heart that I can predict for myself harmony, health, peace, prosperity, and success in business. I enthrone the concepts of peace, harmony, guidance, success, and prosperity in my mind now. I know and believe these thoughts (seeds) will grow and manifest themselves in my experience. I am a gardener; as I sow, so shall I reap. I sow God-like thoughts (seeds), and these wonderful seeds of success, harmony, prosperity, peace, and good will automatically will bring forth a wonderful harvest. I nourish and sustain these seeds regu-

larly and systematically by thinking with interest on them. I know my subconscious mind is a bank which multiplies and magnifies whatever I deposit. I will draw out the fruit of the wonderful seeds I am depositing now. I make these thoughts real by feeling the reality of them. I believe in the law of increase in the same manner that seeds deposited in the soil come forth multiplied 30-fold, 60-fold, and 100-fold. Like seeds, my thoughts dwell in the darkness of my subconscious mind, and, like the seeds, they come above the ground (become objectified) as conditions, experiences, and events. I think frequently on these things, and God's power is with my thoughts of good. God giveth the increase.

When fear or worry thoughts came to this broker, he immediately supplanted them by affirming, "God giveth the increase along all lines." At the end of a month, he was back in his old stride, having more business than he could handle, and employing three extra salesmen.

How She Passed Her Examination

A young college girl, who comes to my public lectures on the powers of your subconscious mind, told me how she overcame fear at her recent examination when her knees were shaking with fear. She decided to overcome the fear by reasoning out in her mind that her fear was a signal to do something. She made up her mind to overcome this fear and she said to herself, "The Lord is my shepherd. God can't be afraid. God is right here. God is my peace and my strength. His river of peace flows through me. God's love indwells me and casts out all fear. I am at peace. The poise and harmony of God is here. I am relaxed, and I answer all questions in Divine order. Infinite Intelligence reveals to me everything I need to know."

She moved to the opposite. She practiced the law of substitution; she supplanted her fear by her faith in God and the good. She did not stay frozen at the end of the pendulum of fear, and thereby she conquered her fear and passed her examination with very high marks.

Fear Thoughts Can't Hurt You

Fear thoughts, worry thoughts, negative thoughts of any kind will not hurt you unless you entertain them for a long period of time and emotionalize them deeply; otherwise, they will not hurt you in the slightest. They are potential trouble for you, but as yet they are not actualized. Your fears cannot be actualized unless you emotionalize them, thereby impressing your subconscious mind, and whatever is impressed in the subconscious mind will come to pass.

Become a Spiritual Giant

Your fear is an aggressive, domineering thought or idea that brags about its power and intimidates, bullies, browbeats, and frightens you into submission of its unrighteous reign. Perhaps you are afraid to meet this gangster in your mind. Maybe you are afraid of the results, and you hesitate to meet this sinister gangster and rout him out.

Fear is a shadow of the mind held by ignorance and darkness. When you hold your fear up to the light of reason and intelligence, it cannot stand the light, and it disappears.

Your state of mind is your master. It is foolish to let that ignorant, blind, stupid monster *fear* push you around and direct your activities. Consider yourself too smart, too brilliant for that to happen. Your faith in God is greater than fear. Fear is faith upside down. Fear is a conglomeration of dark and sinister shadows in the mind. In short, fear is faith in the wrong thing. Become a spiritual giant, call forth confidence in God, and summon His force and power.

When you go forth in the assurance that "one with God is a majority," you will find yourself watched over and guided in every way, and you will became the inevitable victor.

Lost in the Jungle

When I was about ten years of age, I was lost in the jungle. At first I was terrified; then I began to claim that God would lead me out and take care of me. I was immediately seized with an overpowering hunch to travel in a certain direction. This inner push or tendency of the subconscious—which I followed—proved to be correct, and I was miraculously led into the arms of a searching party after two days' time. This *lead* was the prompting of my subconscious mind which knew the way out of the jungle.

In using your subconscious mind, remember that it reasons deductively. It sees the end only, thereby bringing to a logical, sequential conclusion the nature of the premise in the conscious mind.

Don't Fight Fear

Don't fight fear with fear; instead, meet it with a direct declaration of God's Presence and Power, which renders fear powerless. Say to yourself, "The Lord is the strength of my life; of whom should I be afraid?"

Are you afraid of some disease which has gripped you? You will notice that an erroneous thought in your mind can brag and boast of its pseudo strength, and it intimidates you. Don't let such thoughts bully and browbeat you. Meet and subdue them now. Realize that all disease is manufactured by your own mind; it is not something you catch on the outside.

You can change your mind by realizing that the Infinite Healing Presence which made your body is healing it now. As you do this consciously and knowingly, there will be a rearrangement of the thought patterns in your subconscious, and a healing will follow. Your present conviction determines your future and your experience.

The Enemy in Her Own Mind

A young woman said to me recently, "I'm so mad, I could kill Mary!" It seems Mary had spread lies about her and had tried to undermine her in the position she held. The woman permitted Mary to disturb her; she gave to Mary power which Mary did not possess. The trouble was in her own thought-life. Mary was not responsible for the way she was thinking about her, and she realized suddenly that the whole trouble was in her own mental imagery and thought patterns. She felt fear run riot in her mind, intimidating, bullying, and frightening her—the whole process being one of her own creation. The enemy (fear) was really of her own making.

She decided to chop off the head of this fear-thought with the sword of spiritual reason. She saturated her mind with the simple truth, "God is, and His Presence fills my soul and rules my life." She refused to permit Mary to give her migraine, indigestion, insomnia, and the jitters. She realized the power was in her own thought-life and that she was the one who determined how her thoughts moved. It dawned on her that no one had the power to upset her or to take away her faith and confidence in God and all things good.

This woman had a complete healing of the mind, and her favorite prayer was as follows: "God in action in my life brings me beauty, peace, Divine right place, and harmony. I am the offspring of the Infinite and a child of Eternity. I draw close to God, my Heavenly Father. He loves me and cares for me. As I turn to Him, He turns to me; then the dawn appears and all the shadows flee away."

Love's Healing Balm

The following is a wonderful prayer for casting out fear. Affirm these truths frequently, and you will find that an inner sense of peace and tranquility will come over you.

> The love of God flows through me now; I am surrounded by the peace of God, and all is well. Divine love surrounds, enfolds, and encompasses me. This Infinite love is inscribed in my heart and written in my inward parts. I radiate love in thought, words, and deeds. Love unifies and harmonizes all the powers, attributes, and qualities of God within me. Love means joy, peace, freedom, bliss, and praise. Love is freedom. It opens prison doors and sets free all the captives. I am radiating love towards all, for everyone represents the love of God. I salute the Divinity in the other. I know and believe that Divine love heals me now. Love is a guiding principle in me; it brings into my experience perfect, harmonious relationships. God is love. *"He that dwelleth in love, dwelleth in God, and God in him."*

BASIC POINTS TO REMEMBER

1. Love is an emotional attachment. Love must have an object.
2. If you really want to banish fear, you must give up your jealousies, hatreds, peeves, and grudges.
3. Get a new estimate and blueprint of yourself. Fall in love with your Greater Self.
4. Love of God means that you are mentally and emotionally tied with that which is lovely, pure, noble, and God-like. You honor only one Power.
5. Love is faith and loyalty to God. Fear is faith in the wrong thing. Fear is a shadow in the mind. Love and fear can't dwell together.
6. A jealous person is full of fear and feels insecure and unworthy. Love and trust cast out jealousy.
7. Your subconscious magnifies everything you deposit in it. Deposit love, faith, confidence, laughter, and good will.
8. When your knees are shaking with fear, overcome the fear by realizing God can't be afraid, and you are one with God.
9. Fear thoughts can't hurt you except you indulge them and emotionalize them.
10. Fear is a thought you allow in your mind which browbeats and intimidates you. Enthrone love and faith in God in your mind.
11. When lost in the jungles of the earth or in a mental

jungle of confusion and fear, realize that God knows the way out. He will answer you.

12. Don't fight fear with fear. Meet it with a direct declaration: "God is the only Presence and the only Power, and there is nothing to fear."

13. Chop off the head of your fear-thought with the sword of spiritual reason.

14. *"He that dwelleth in love, dwelleth in God, and God in him."*

Law

10

The
℗ositive 𝕷aw
of emotional control

The an-
cient Greeks said, "Man, know thyself." As you study yourself,
you seem to be made up of four parts: Your physical body,
emotional nature, intellect, and spiritual nature.

You are placed here to so discipline yourself that your intellectual, emotional, and physical natures are completely aligned,
controlled, and directed along God-like ways.

Your physical body has no initiative of itself, no self-conscious
intelligence, and no volition in and of itself. It is completely
subject to your commands or decrees. Look upon your body as
a great disc upon which you play your emotions and beliefs.
Being a disc, on which impressions of all sorts can be made, it

will faithfully record all your emotionalized concepts and will never deviate from them; therefore, you can register upon it a melody of love and beauty, or one of grief and sorrow.

Resentment, jealousy, hatred, anger, and melancholia all are expressed in the body as various diseases. As you learn to control your mental and emotional nature, you will become a channel for the Divine, and you will release the imprisoned splendor concealed within you.

Becoming Emotionally Mature

Think over this for a moment: You cannot buy a healthy body with all the money in the world, but you can nevertheless acquire health through the riches of the mind, such as thoughts of peace, harmony, and perfect health.

It is absolutely essential for you to control your emotions if you want to become emotionally and spiritually mature. You are considered emotionally mature when you release your feelings constructively and harmoniously. If you do not discipline or bridle your emotions, you are considered emotionally immature and not grown up, even though chronologically you may be fifty years old.

Getting the Right Concept of Yourself

The greatest tyrant is a false idea which controls your mind and holds you in bondage. The ideas you hold about yourself induce definite emotions within you. Psychologically speaking, emotions control your course along life's path for good or evil.

If you are full of resentment toward someone or are possessed by a grudge, these emotions will exert an evil influence over you and will govern your actions in a manner which will be exceedingly different from what you may honestly desire. When you want to be friendly, affable, and cordial, you will be ugly, cynical, and sour. When you want to be healthy, successful, and prosperous in life, you will find everything going wrong.

Those of you who are reading this book are aware of your capacity to choose a concept of peace and good will. Sincerely accept the ideas of peace and love in your mind, and you will be governed, controlled, and guided accordingly.

How She Overcame Depression

A mother, whose only child had died, was grief-stricken. She was so deeply affected that her grief was affecting her vision, and she suffered from migraine headaches. She fell into a deep state of depression and melancholia. This woman was a former nurse, so I suggested to her that she go to a hospital and offer her services in the children's ward. She followed my advice, and, in offering her time at a local hospital, she began to pour out love on the children; she coddled, cossetted, and fed them. Her love no longer was bottled up within her; she again had someone who needed her, and she began to release the emotion of love along constructive channels.

She practiced what is called "sublimation" by redirecting in God-like ways the energy that was locked up in her subconscious mind. In this manner she drained off all the poison pockets in her deeper mind, and she became joyous, happy, radiant, and free.

How She Overcame Bad Temper

A woman who attended my public lectures on the power of the subconscious mind told me that she was periodically accustomed to fits of temper and anger by the actions of her neighbors. Instead of letting the anger and hatred affect her mentally and physically by pushing it back into the subconscious, however, she transmuted it into muscular energy by getting a gallon of water and washing the windows and the floor. Sometimes she would dig in her garden, saying aloud to herself, "I am digging in the garden of God and planting God's ideas." She would do this for fifteen minutes at a time. When washing the windows, she would say aloud, "I am cleansing my mind with the waters of love and life." This woman adopted a simple but effective method of working off her negative emotions in a physical way.

His Mental Photograph

I once had an interesting chat with a young man who had studied mental discipline in Paris, France. His procedure was to take, as he said, "a good look at or mental photograph of" his thoughts, sensations, moods, reactions, and his tone of voice. Then he would say of the negatives: "These are not of God; they are destructive and false. I will mentally turn to God within me and think from the standpoint of wisdom, truth, and beauty." He made a habit of this. He would stop when he got angry and say to himself, "This is not the Infinite thinking, speaking, and acting in me. I now think, speak, and act from the standpoint of God and His love."

Every time this young man was prone to get angry, critical, depressed, or irritable, he would think of God and His love and peace. This is internal discipline and spiritual understanding.

You Can Control Your Emotions

Let us see how our emotions are generated. Suppose that you observe a cripple; perhaps you are moved to the emotion of pity. On the other hand, you might look at your young, beautiful child, and you feel the emotion of love welling up within you.

You know that you cannot imagine an emotion, but if you imagine an unpleasant episode or event of the past, you will thereby induce the corresponding emotion. Remember that it is essential first to entertain a thought or mental image before you can induce an emotion.

An emotion always is the working out of an idea in your mind. If you sincerely wish to govern and to control your emotions, you must maintain control over your thoughts and mental images.

By taking charge of your thoughts, you *can* substitute love for fear, good will for ill will, joy for sadness, and peace for irritation. The instant you receive the stimulus of a negative emotion, supplant it with the mood of love and good will. Instead of giving way to fear, say to yourself, "One with God is a majority." Fill your mind with the concepts of faith, confidence, peace, and love; then the negative thoughts cannot enter in.

The Emotion of Love Freed Him

A pilot who had just returned from South Vietnam told me that when he was seized with fear while flying over the enemy lines, he would say to himself over and over again, "God's love surrounds me and all the other men and envelops this plane. His love is my guide and my direction. He watches over us, and we are in His Presence."

This affirmation impressed his mind with the feeling of love and faith. This mood of love supplanted his fear. ". . . *Perfect love casteth out fear.*" (I John 4:18)

How Your Emotions Affect Your Body

Have you noticed the effect of fear upon your face, eyes, heart, and other organs? You know the effect on your digestive tract of bad news or grief. Observe the change that takes place when it is found that the bad news is groundless.

All negative emotions are destructive and depress the vital forces of the body. A chronic worrier usually has trouble with digestion. If something very pleasant occurs in his experience, his digestion becomes normal, because normal circulation is restored and the necessary gastric secretions no longer are interfered with.

The way to overcome and discipline your emotions is not through repression or suppression. When you repress an emotion, the energy accumulates in your subconscious mind and remains snarled there. This occurs in the same manner as the pressure increases in a boiler when all the valves are closed and the heat of the fire is increased; finally there will be an explosion.

Today in the field of psychosomatics it is being discovered that many cases of ill health, such as arthritis, asthma, cardiac troubles, and even failures in life, are due to suppressed or repressed emotions which may have occurred during early life or childhood. These repressed or suppressed emotions rise like ghosts to haunt you later on, and in the next paragraphs you will learn how to become free of them for the rest of your life.

The Positive Emotions of Faith and Confidence

There is a spiritual and psychological way to follow in banishing the repressed or suppressed emotions inhabiting the gloomy gallery of your mind. The ideal way to rid yourself of these emotions is to practice the law of substitution.

Through the law of mental substitution, you substitute a positive, constructive thought for a negative thought. When negative thoughts enter your mind, do not fight them; just say to yourself: "My faith is in God and all things good. His love watches over me at all times;" you will find that the negative thoughts disappear just as light dispels the darkness.

If you are disturbed, anxious, or worried, meditate on the words of the Psalms and affirm:

> *The Lord is my shepherd; I shall not want.* (Ps. 23:1)
> *. . . I will fear no evil: for thou art with me . . .* (Ps. 23:4)
> *God is . . . a very present help in trouble.* (Ps. 46:1)
> *The Lord is my light and my salvation; whom shall I fear? the Lord is the strength of my life; of whom shall I be afraid?* (Ps. 27:1)

As you mentally dwell on these great truths, you will generate inevitably the positive emotions of faith and confidence which neutralize and destroy any negative emotion.

Watch Your Reactions

I recently said to a man who was complaining of ulcers and high blood pressure, "Have you observed your typical reactions to people, newspaper articles, business associates, and radio commentators? Have you noticed your usual stereotyped behavior?"

He replied, "No, I have not noticed these things." He was taking himself for granted and was not growing spiritually. He began to think about his reactions; then he admitted that many of the current news articles and television commentators irritated him immensely. He said that he often had written them vitriolic and abusive letters.

This man had reacted in a machine-like manner, and he had not disciplined himself. I explained to him that it made no difference if all the writers and commentators were wrong and he, alone, was right; his negative emotion was destructive and it was robbing him of vitality, health, and peace of mind.

He came to a conclusion in his mind that, from this moment forward, he would give all congressmen, writers, commentators, and newscasters the freedom and the right to say and to write what they believed was true, and he gave them the perfect right and freedom to express themselves according to the inner dictates of their hearts. He also decided that it was perfectly reasonable to assume that they would grant him the complete freedom and right to write articles or letters to the newspapers and columnists which were in complete disagreement with what they said and wrote. He realized that this was a sign of emotional maturity and that it had been childish for him to have resented and hated those who had disagreed with his views.

The simple prayer formula adopted by him was this: "From this moment forward, I will think right, feel right, act right, do right, and be right. I will think, speak, write, and react from the Divine Center within me and not from the superimposed structure of false beliefs, prejudices, bigotry, and ignorance. From the depths of my heart, I wish for all men the right to life, liberty, and the pursuit of happiness, and I practice the Golden Rule and the Law of Love."

This man's ulcers and high blood pressure disappeared within a few weeks, and his physician's tests indicated a complete healing. His changed attitude changed everything.

You Are Living in Two Worlds

You are living in an external and an internal world; yet they both are one. One is visible and the other invisible (objective and subjective). Your external world enters through your five senses and is shared by everyone. Your internal world of thoughts, feelings, imagination, sensations, beliefs, and reactions is invisible and belongs to you alone.

Ask yourself, "In which world do I live? Do I live in the world that is revealed by my five senses, or in the inner world?" It is in this inner world that you live all the time; this is where you feel and suffer.

Suppose that you are invited to a banquet. Everything there that you see, hear, taste, smell, and touch belongs to the external world. All that you think, feel, like, and dislike belongs to your inner world. You actually attend two banquets, which are recorded differently: namely, one the outer, and one the inner. It is your inner world of thought, feeling, and emotion in which you rise and fall and sway to and fro.

How to Transform Yourself

In order to transform yourself, you must begin to change your inner world through the purification of your emotions and by the correct ordering of your mind through right thinking. If you want to grow spiritually, you must transform yourself.

Transformation means the changing of one thing into another. There are many well-known transformations of matter. Through a process of chemistry, sugar is changed into alcohol; radium slowly changes into lead. The food that you eat is transformed stage by stage into all the substances necessary for your existence.

Your experiences, coming in as impressions, must be similarly transformed. Suppose that you see a person whom you love and admire; you receive certain impressions about him. Suppose on the other hand that you meet a person whom you dislike; you also receive impressions but of a different type. Your husband or daughter, sitting on the couch as you read this, is to you what you conceive him or her to be. In other words, impressions are received by your *mind*. If you were deaf, you would not hear their voices.

You can change your impressions of people. To transform your impression is to transform yourself. In order to change your life, change your reactions to life. Do you find yourself reacting in stereotyped ways? If your reactions are negative, you will find yourself sick, morose, morbid, and depressed. Never permit your life to be a series of negative reactions to the impressions that come to you every day.

In order to truly transform yourself, you must reverse every negative thought by claiming that God's love fills your mind and heart, and, as you make a habit of this, you will become a better man morally, intellectually, and physically. "He who rises from prayer a better man, his prayer is answered." (George Meredith)

You have a panacea for every trouble. *"Come unto me, all ye that labour and are heavy laden, and I will give you rest."* (Matthew 11:28)

"If in this life we would enjoy the peace of God, we must make our heart a spiritual temple, and whenever we find our thought and feeling wandering away from Him on any occasion, we must bring it back to the contemplation of His Holy Presence." (Brother Lawrence) "The thoughts of his heart, these are the wealth of a man." (Burmese saying)

Prayer for Controlling the Emotions

"He that is slow to wrath is of great understanding: but he that is hasty of spirit exalteth folly." (Proverbs 14:29) I am always poised, serene, and calm. The peace of God floods my mind and my whole being. I practice the Golden Rule and sincerely wish peace and good will to all men.

I know that the love of all things which are good penetrates my mind and casts out all fear. I am now living in the joyous expectancy of the best. My mind is free from all worry and doubt. My words of truth now dissolve every negative thought and emotion within me. I forgive everyone; I open the doorway of my heart to God's Presence. My whole being is flooded with the light and understanding from within.

The petty things of life no longer irritate me. When fear, worry, and doubt knock at my door, faith in goodness, truth, and beauty opens the door, and there is no one there. *"O, God, Thou art my God, and there is none else."*

THINGS TO WATCH

1. You are here to discipline your thoughts, feelings, and reactions to life.
2. You become emotionally mature as you think, speak, act, and respond from your Divine Center or the God-Self within you.
3. The greatest tyrant is a false idea which controls your mind and holds you in bondage. Immediately supplant it with a new concept of yourself.
4. Love is an emotional attachment; it is outgoing. Pour out love and good will, and you will neutralize all the negative emotions snarled up in your subconscious.
5. You can transmute bad temper into constructive muscular energy by washing windows, playing a game of handball, or digging in your garden.
6. When you get angry, stop and affirm, "I am going to think, speak, and act from the standpoint of wisdom, truth, beauty, and love."
7. You can control your emotional reaction to people by identifying yourself with the Presence of God in each person. Substitute love for hate.
8. Faith in God and all things good casts out fear.
9. Suppressed or repressed emotions bring on all manner of bodily diseases. Become a channel for God and release all your emotions in God-like ways.
10. Substitute a positive, constructive thought for a negative one. The positive emotion of faith and

confidence will neutralize and destroy all negative emotions.

11. How do you mentally and emotionally react to events, conditions, and circumstances? It is your reaction that determines your emotion. Think right, feel right, be right, and do right. No one can disturb you but yourself. Your thought is incipient action. Think God's thoughts, and God's power is with your thoughts of good.

12. You are living in two worlds: the internal world of your thoughts, feelings, imagery, beliefs, and opinions, and the objective world from which are conveyed impressions to you through your five senses. You live in the inner world of your thoughts, feelings, and beliefs. The inner controls the outer.

13. In order to transform yourself, you must purify your emotions through right thinking. Emotion follows thought.

14. To change your life, change your reaction to life. If you were blind and deaf, you could not see or hear people, and you would respond and react differently to them. See God in the other, and:

> What thou seest, man,
> That too become thou must;
> God if thou seest God, and
> Dust if thou seest dust.

The
𝕿hrilling 𝕷aw
of marital harmony

Poet Ralph Waldo Emerson claimed that marriage has deep and serious benefits, and great joys. Oliver Goldsmith said, "I chose my wife, as she did her wedding gown, for qualities that would wear well."

Marriage is the holiest of all earthly unions, and it should be entered into reverently and prayerfully, with full understanding of its sacredness. The sanctity of marriage and the family relation constitute the real cornerstone of our society and civilization.

Marriage, to be complete, must be on a spiritual basis. The contemplation of Divine ideals, the study of the laws of life, and a conscious unity in thought, purpose, plan, and action bring about that wedded bliss, that holy union which makes the outer life like the inner: peaceful, joyous, and harmonious.

Love Unites and Fear Divides

Mrs. Jones lived in constant fear that her husband would desert her. Her fear was a negative feeling which was subconsciously communicated to her husband. This man was not acquainted with the laws of the conscious and subconscious minds, and her conviction that he would leave her was felt by him at his subjective level.

One morning, her husband said to her, "I feel that you want me to leave. I had a dream in which you appeared and said, 'Leave the house. I don't want you any more, so please go away.'"

She immediately told her husband of her fear, however, and explained to him that his subconscious mind simply had dramatized in a very vivid manner her own fears and anxieties. He understood perfectly. Night after night prior to sleep, she supplanted her fear by picturing her husband as radiant, happy, prosperous, and successful. She radiated the mood of love, peace, and good will to him many times a day, feeling and claiming that he was good, kind, and loving, and that he was a tremendous success.

Her mood of fear changed to a mood of love and peace. She had discovered a great truth: that love brings about an unbroken unity in married life.

The Truth Set Him Free

The late Dr. Hester Brunt of Capetown, South Africa, once introduced me to a man after one of my lectures in that city.

She told me that this man had served a term in an English prison and, after his release, had entered the banking business in Johannesburg, South Africa. He had married a very prominent woman and had been blessed with two wonderful sons. He lived in constant fear, though, that his wife and his sons would discover his past, that he would be exposed by the press, and that his wife would thereupon immediately divorce him. He was afraid that this ugly publicity would ruin the future of his two sons. This man's chronic worry and anxiety had caused him to become seriously ill, resulting in frequent emotional outbursts and tantrums toward his wife and sons.

I sensed that something was very wrong, as the man's physician could not persuade him to accept either injections or oral medications. I asked him, "What is eating you inside?"

He told me about his error and resultant imprisonment for two years in England. Having been thoroughly briefed by Dr. Brunt and the man's wife, I explained to him that his wife and sons, Dr. Brunt, and the bank officials had known all about the mistakes of his earlier life for a long time! As a matter of fact, his wife had known about his past prior to having married him, but she never had mentioned it to him as she knew that he had become a transformed man and she did not want to hurt his feelings. He had made good and his past was a closed book.

When the truth was revealed to him that all the people who really mattered in his life knew all about his past and loved him for what he was now, he astounded his doctor by recovering almost immediately. His suffering and sickness had been due to a distorted mental image. The transformation of his mind resulted in a perfect, harmonious, and peaceful relationship with his wife and sons.

The Secret of Her Freedom

On a recent trip to the beautiful island of Hawaii, I met a very attractive young lady who confided in me that she was going to break her engagement to a wealthy businessman because she was terrified of an ocean voyage. Her fiancé already had made extensive plans for a honeymoon trip around the world on his private yacht. She said, "I am deathly afraid to tell him; I am abashed and ashamed. I simply can't tell him. I will return his ring with a note."

I explained to her how to solve her dilemma and gain her freedom from her abnormal fear of the ocean. I gave her a seaman's version of the Twenty-Third Psalm and suggested that for ten minutes, three times a day, she affirm out loud this particular version of the Psalm. I explained to her how these spiritual vibrations would destroy all of the negative forces of fear, worry, and anxiety that were presently lodged in her subconscious mind.

Seaman's Version of the 23rd Psalm [6]

The Lord is my Pilot; I shall not drift. He lighteth me across the dark waters; He steereth me in the deep channels; He keepeth my log. He guideth me by the star of holiness for His name's sake. Yea, though I sail 'mid the thunders and tempests of life, I shall dread no danger; for Thou art with me. Thy love and Thy care they shelter me. Thou preparest a harbor before me in the homeland of eternity; Thou anointest the waves with oil; my ship rideth calmly. Surely, sunlight and starlight

---

[6] By J. Rogers, a merchant marine captain, written during World War II. Published by Navy Chaplains Bulletin, Washington, D.C.

shall favor me on the voyage I take, and I will rest in the port of my God forever.

The young woman followed my instructions to the letter and succeeded in impressing these truths in her subconscious mind with feeling and understanding; all her fear vanished. She had supplanted her fear with faith in God as her pilot. She now has a new lease on life. Her fear was a shadow in her mind, and when the Light came into her mind, the darkness disappeared.

He Demanded a Divorce

Consider the case of May, who had been married for forty years. She had worked with her husband in his business, had helped it grow, and had borne him four children. Suddenly, one day he demanded a divorce so that he could marry a cousin of his. May felt crushed, depressed, and full of foreboding about the future. May discovered that she didn't have to feel dejected and depressed. She learned how to use the powers of her mind by faithfully practicing the techniques outlined in these pages, and she found an amazing source of strength, inspiration, and courage.

She sold the business and took a trip around the world. She affirmed frequently, "Infinite Intelligence attracts to me a man with whom I harmonize perfectly." During her trip, she met the ideal man for her and eventually married him in Paris. May won the respect, loyalty, and devotion of her children and her neighbors. She had realized that her divorce had brought about an entry into a richer, grander, nobler, and more God-like life. She had learned to meet the challenge of despair and loneliness with confidence and trust in the infinite wisdom of her subconscious mind.

Married Five Times

A young woman, aged twenty-eight, once said to me, "This is my fifth marriage, and this husband is worse than the preceding four! I will have my final decree of divorce from him within a few months."

She was bitter and resentful toward her former husbands. I explained to her though that remarrying without forgiveness would cause her to attract similar type men, and each one progressively worse as her resentment and hostility became magnified in her subconscious mind. All the while, she had not known that her inner mood of resentment and hostility was causing her to attract men who were the affinities of her deeper mind. Unconsciously, she was operating the law of attraction. Like attracts like, and birds of a feather do flock together.

The cure thus was to set herself and her former husbands free by forgiving (giving for) herself the mood of love and peace for the mood of resentment. She released all her former husbands by affirming boldly: "I release you and let you go, wishing for you health, wealth, love, happiness, peace, and joy." Her ideas of love and marriage changed, and she began to lift love to a spiritual basis. She realized that her previous attitudes and motives for marriage were all wrong. She prayed as follows:

> I know that I am one with God now. In Him I live, move, and have my being. God is life; this life is the life of all men and women. We are all sons and daughters of the one Father. I know and believe that there is a man waiting to love and cherish me. I know I can contribute to his happiness and peace. He loves my ideals, and I love his ideals. He does not want to make me over; neither do I want to make him over. There are mutual love, freedom, and respect.

> There is one mind; I know him now in this mind. I now unite with the qualities and attributes that I admire and want expressed by my husband. I am one with them in my mind. We know and love each other in Divine Mind. I see the God in him; he sees the God in me. Having met him *within*, I must meet him in the *without*, for this is the law of my own mind.
>
> These words go forth and accomplish whereunto they are sent. I know it is now done, finished, and accomplished in God. Thank you, Father.

A few weeks later she had occasion to have a wisdom tooth removed. A beautiful friendship developed with the dentist. Eventually he proposed marriage—as she said, "right out of the blue"—and she added, "I knew intuitively he was the man about whom I had prayed. It was a case of love at first sight." The author performed their marriage ceremony, and I must say it was a real spiritual union of two people seeking their way back to the heart of God.

How He Found His Ideal

A man once said to me in Rochester, New York, that a woman with whom he had been going for three years refused to marry him and that he was going to commit suicide if he could not have her. I taught him how to pray for a wife in the following manner:

> God is one and indivisible. In Him we live, move, and have our being. I know and believe that God indwells every person; I am one with God and with all people. I now attract the right woman who is in complete accord with me. This is a spiritual union, because it is the spirit of God functioning through the personality of someone with whom I blend perfectly. I know I can give to this woman love, light, and truth. I know I can make this woman's life full, complete, and wonderful.

I now decree that she possesses the following qualities and attributes: i.e., she is spiritual, loyal, faithful, and true. She is harmonious, peaceful, and happy. We are irresistibly attracted to each other. Only that which belongs to love, truth, and wholeness can enter my experience. I accept my ideal companion now.

He continued mentally and emotionally to unite with these truths every night and morning until such time as he had subjectively absorbed them. After a few weeks, he met a waitress in a hotel where he was staying; he fell in love with her and married her. It was an ideal union.

What about the woman without whom he could not live? In the interim, it was revealed to him through friends that she already had been married six times—and never had taken the trouble to get a divorce! She also was an ex-convict and had a police record for several crimes. Even while she was keeping company with him, she had been living with another man.

That's the Man I Want

A legal secretary in London, England, said to me during an interview, "I am in love with my boss. He is married and has four children, but I don't care. I'm going to get him and snare him away, even though he doesn't want to leave his wife."

She seemed perfectly willing to break up their home in order to gain her point. However, I explained to this young woman that she really did not want this married man; that what she desired deep down in her heart was to be married, to have children, and to be loved, cherished, and admired; and that actually she could attract a man free from all encumbrances who would be the ideal mate for her. To achieve this desire, prayer was her answer.

I pointed out to her that she might succeed in possessing this man and forcing him to her will and her way, but that inevitably more problems and difficulties would result, as she would have impregnated herself with limitation and a sense of guilt. *"Thou shalt not covet thy neighbor's wife . . ."* (Exodus 20:17) I gently reminded her of this great law: ". . . *Whatsoever ye would that men should do to you, do ye even so to them . . ."* (Matthew 7:12) This commandment gives the whole law of a happy and successful life. In selfishness and greed, this is forgotten.

The following questions caused a great awakening in the mind and heart of this young secretary: "What would you like the family of the man, whom you weaned away from his wife, to think of you? How do you want them to feel about you?" I answered these questions for her by saying to her, "You would want his wife and his family to think of you as a noble, gentle, dignified lady who is honest, sincere, and upright. Apply this principle and see if you still desire to wreck their home."

She saw the truth at once, and she wept copiously. She agreed that she could attract an ideal companion without causing grief or pain to anyone else. She prayed by affirming: "I am now attracting a wonderful man who harmonizes with me spiritually, mentally, and physically. He comes to me without encumbrances and in Divine order."

Shortly thereafter she met a young chemist at the London Truth Forum in Caxton Hall, London, which she had begun to attend at my suggestion. This young woman had discovered that there is a law of mind which will bring to pass whatever she would accept as true.

Love Is a Oneness

Suppose that a man cheats on his wife. If he had love and respect for his wife, he would not want any other woman. When man has found his true, spiritual ideal in marriage, he has no desire for any other woman. Love is a oneness; it is not a duality or a multiplicity.

A man who runs around with many women—who represent the many adulterous moods within him—is "marrying" (mentally and emotionally uniting with) many concepts, such as frustration, resentment, cynicism, etc. When a man has found love with his mate, he has found fullness of life. If a man cheats on his wife, therefore, he is frustrated and never really has experienced ideal love, or a feeling of oneness. He has an inferiority complex plus, undoubtedly, a guilt complex.

Inevitably, the women he meets are vacillating, neurotic, and confused; he is seeing and hearing his own inner vibration. The women he meets are just as frustrated and unstable as himself. Birds of a feather flock together. Like begets like.

Avoid a Dead-End Street

Once a woman said to me, "I have been going with a married man for four years, and I love him dearly. I can't give him up. What shall I do?" She had failed to acquire a husband or proper boy-friend because she did not know how to pray; she got a pseudo satisfaction, or false thrill, from stealing another woman's husband. She had a profound inferiority complex, and she was generally very unstable.

I explained to her that her type of conduct usually ended up in a blind alley or a dead-end street, accompanied by sedatives and tranquilizers and only too often an overdose of sleeping tablets. I pointed out to her that the man would continue to use her body until such time as he got tired of her, but would never marry her, and that she was getting older and wasting her time.

What she really wanted was to be married, to be called "Mrs.," to have a home, and to be respected by her neighbors, friends, and relatives. The answer to her problem was prayer. She immediately severed relationship with the married man, and she practiced the prayer on how to attract the ideal husband as given previously in this chapter.

As a result she is now happily married and is genuinely grateful for having discovered the inner powers of her mind.

Should I Get a Divorce?

A frequent question propounded to me is, "Should I get a divorce?" Now this is an individual problem and it cannot be generalized. In some cases divorce is not the solution—no more so than marriage is necessarily the solution for a lonely man.

Divorce may be right for one person and wrong for another. A divorced woman may be far more noble and God-like than many of her married sisters who are living a lie rather than facing the truth.

In some cases, there never was a real marriage in the first place. Because a man and woman have a marriage license and live in a house, it does not follow that it is a real home. Perhaps it is a place of discord and hate. When children are present and the parents refuse to radiate love, peace, and good will to each other, it is better to dissolve such a union than to have the mood of hate warp the minds of the youngsters. Many times a child's life and mind are permanently affected by the mood of the parents which results in neurosis, delinquency, and crime. It is far better for a boy to live with one parent who loves him than it is for him to live with two who hate each other and fight all the time.

Where there is no love, freedom, or respect between husband and wife, such a marriage is a farce, a sham, and a masquerade, because God (Love) has not joined them together. God is Love, and the heart is the chamber of God's Presence; when two hearts are joined together in mutual love, that is a real marriage because Love has joined them together.

Get a New Estimate of Yourself

Man demotes himself by feeling his lack. His fear is transmitted to his wife; she reacts in kind. She cannot see him in the way she formerly did, as he has not the same feeling about himself. She can see him only in the way he sees himself; likewise, he can see her only in the way she sees herself.

If a man feels himself to be dignified, he commands respect, and he gets it. A man who has the predominant mood of success and happiness knits together all the members of his household. He is a cementing influence. Harmony and peace reign supreme in the household. Your dominant conviction makes others see what you see.

Becoming a Successful Husband or Wife

When you married your husband or wife, you must have admired certain of his or her characteristics, virtues, and qualities. Identify with the good qualities and exalt them. Cease being a scavenger by dwelling on the shortcomings of each other. Make a list of his or her good points, and give your attention and devotion to them. As you do this, your marriage will grow more blessed and beautiful through the years.

The Biblical Formula

"*. . . What therefore God hath joined together, let not man put asunder.*" (Matthew 19:6) This biblical formula reveals to you that in order for a marriage to be real, it must first be spiritual; it must be of the heart.

If both your hearts are moved by love, sincerity, and honesty, then that is God joining both of you together; truly, it is the marriage made in heaven, which means harmony and understanding. You know and feel that the action of your heart is love, and God is Love.

God is not present in all marriages; perhaps there were ulterior motives in the union. If a man marries a woman for money, for position, or to satisfy his ego, that marriage is false; it is a lie. If a woman marries a man for security, wealth, position, a thrill, or to get even with someone else, such a marriage is not of God; for God, or the Truth, was not present. Such marriages are not real because they are not based on love. Honesty, integrity, and respect are born of love.

Where there is a real, true, heavenly marriage—a union of hearts, minds, and bodies—there can be no divorce. Neither do they seek divorce, for it is a spiritual union; it is a union of two hearts; they are united in love. "*. . . What therefore God hath joined together, let not man put asunder.*"

Marriage Prayer for Husband and Wife

We are gathered together in the Presence of God. There is but One God, One Life, One Law, One Mind, and One Father—our Father. We are united in love, harmony, and peace. I rejoice in the peace, happiness, and success of my mate. God is guiding each one of us at all times. We speak to each other from the standpoint of the Divine Center within us. Our words to each other are as a honeycomb, sweet to the ear and pleasant to the bones. We identify with the good qualities of each other and constantly exalt them.

The Love of God flows through us to all in our household and to all people everywhere. We believe and know that the Omnipresent Power and Intelligence of the Infinite One moves through each one of us and all members of our household, and that we are positively, definitely, physically and mentally healed. We know that Divine right action is taking place in every cell, organ, tissue, and function of each one of us, manifesting as peace, harmony, and health.

We believe that Divine guidance is now being experienced by everyone in this household. God—the Great Counselor—leads each one of us to ways of pleasantness and paths of peace.

The words which we speak now shall accomplish what we please and prosper whereunto they are sent. We rejoice now and enter into the mood of thankfulness, knowing that our prayer of faith is fulfilled.

STEP THIS WAY TO A HAPPY MARRIAGE

1. Marriage is the holiest of all earthly unions. It should be entered into reverently, peacefully, and with a deep understanding of its sacredness.

2. A wife's constant fear can be communicated to the subconscious of her husband and cause endless trouble.

3. The past is dead. The only thing that matters is the present moment. Change your present thought and keep it changed, and you change your destiny. Suffering is due to ignorance and distorted mental pictures.

4. Mentally and emotionally identify yourself with the 23rd Psalm, and you will banish all abnormal fear.

5. Meet the challenge of loneliness and despair with confidence and trust in the infinite wisdom of your subconscious mind.

6. You attract the affinities of your dominant subconscious mood. Forgive yourself and everybody else, and then pray for a Divine companion by building into your mentality the qualities which you admire in a mate.

7. Infinite Intelligence will attract to you the ideal husband or wife if you pray sincerely and trust your deeper mind to bring your request to pass.

8. You must never covet another person's wife or husband. Claim what you want, believe that Life will give it to you, and you shall have it.

9. Love is oneness, and if you are really in love with your husband or wife, you could not want another.

10. A single girl really does not want a married man who has no intention of marrying her. She wants a husband, a home, love, and respect. She must give up the married man (the muddled state) before she can attract what she really wants (the ideal state).

11. Many husbands and wives living together are divorced from love, kindness, peace, harmony, good will, and understanding. Such a marriage is a farce, a sham, and a masquerade. It is better to break up such a lie than to continue living the lie.

12. Man demotes himself by his feeling of lack and inferiority, and his wife usually reacts accordingly.

13. Identify with the good qualities and characteristics of your mate, and your marriage will grow more blessed through the years.

14. ". . . *What therefore God* (Love) *hath joined together, let not man put asunder.*" When love unites two hearts together, there is no divorce, for Love is the knot that binds man and woman in the endless course of life, now and forevermore.

The
Glorious Law
of peace of mind

So serious have the ravages of worry become that this problem enters into countless medical conventions both here and abroad. Millions of people throughout the world are literally sick from worrying. The people who worry always are expecting things to go wrong. Their worry is primarily due to a lack of faith in God. They brood or worry over a great many things that never happen. They will tell you all the reasons why something bad should happen, and not one reason why something good should or could happen. This constant worry debilitates their entire system, resulting in physical and mental disorders.

He Worried About What Had Not Happened

A man said to me, "I'm worried sick about my drug store; I may lose it. Business is good, but it can't last. I worry about going bankrupt. My mind is in a turmoil, and I can't sleep nights."

"Tell me the nature of your business problem, Tom," I suggested.

"Oh, nothing has happened yet, but I fear it *will* happen. I worry myself sick, and I also get my wife upset. How can I stop worrying?"

This man actually was doing a good business; he had a fine bank account, and, by ordinary standards in the drug business, he was prospering. His constant negative thinking was robbing him of vitality, enthusiasm, and energy, and in addition, he was making himself weaker and less able to meet any challenges that might come along.

I explained to this pharmacist that if he continued worrying he would attract the conditions upon which he was mentally dwelling, that the only thing really wrong with him was a false belief in his mind, and that he had forgotten that he personally could control his thoughts and his life. I gave him the following prayer for his business:

> My business is God's business. God is my partner in all of my affairs. God is prospering my business in a wonderful way. I claim that all those working with me in my store are spiritual links in its growth, welfare, and prosperity; I know this, I believe it, and I rejoice in their success and happiness. I solve all my problems by trusting the infinite intelligence within my subconscious mind to reveal to me the answer. I rest in security and peace. I am surrounded by peace, love, and harmony. I know that all my business relationships with people are in accord

with the law of harmony. Infinite Intelligence reveals to me better ways in which I can serve humanity. I know that God indwells all of my customers and clients. I work harmoniously with others to the end that happiness, prosperity, and peace reign supreme. Whenever any worry thoughts come to my mind, I will immediately affirm, *I will fear no evil: for thou art with me.* (Psalm 23:4)

Tom began to set aside ten or fifteen minutes in the morning, afternoon, and evening for the purpose of reiterating these truths, knowing that through their frequent habitation of his mind, he would be reconditioned to constructive thinking. When morbid thoughts came to his mind, he would immediately affirm, "God is with me." He said to me that on one day he must have said "God is with me" about a thousand times.

Gradually the neurotic thought pattern of chronic worry that he had complained of in the beginning, and which had been repeating itself with monotonous regularity, was completely dissipated, and he rejoiced in his freedom in God.

She Healed Her Anxiety Neurosis

I received a letter from a woman in which she wrote, "My husband sits around all day and does nothing but drink beer. He won't work, and he whines all the time. He worries me terribly, and my physician says that I have 'anxiety neurosis.' On top of that, I suffer from asthma, skin trouble, and high blood pressure. My husband is killing me."

I wrote to her and told her that today it is well-known in psychological and medical circles that many skin disorders, asthma, allergies, cardiac disorders, and diabetes as well as a host of other illnesses are brought on by chronic worry—which is another name for her anxiety neurosis. I also gave her a spiritual prescription in which I suggested that several times a day she was to bless her husband as follows:

> My husband is God's man. He is Divinely active, Divinely prospered, peaceful, happy, and joyous. He is expressing himself fully and is in his true place; he receives a marvelous income. Sobriety and peace of mind reign supreme in his life. I now picture him coming home every night and telling me how happy he is in his new job, and I leave it all to God to fulfill.

I enclosed a second prescription which she was to take mentally and emotionally six or seven times a day until her subconscious absorbed it. She also was to picture her doctor telling her that she was whole and perfect. Following is her second prescription:

> The gifts of God are mine. I use every moment of this day to glorify God. God's harmony, peace, and abundance are mine. Divine love flowing from me blesses all who come into my atmosphere. God's love is healing me now. I fear no evil for God is with me. I am always surrounded by the sacred circle of God's love and power. I claim, feel, know, and believe definitely and positively that the spell of God's love and eternal watchfulness guides, heals, and takes care of all members of my family and loved ones.
>
> I forgive everyone, and I sincerely radiate God's love, peace, and good will to all men everywhere. At the center of my being is peace; this is the peace of God. In this stillness I feel His strength, guidance, and the love of His Holy Presence. I am Divinely guided in all my ways. I am a clear channel for God's love, light, truth, and beauty. I feel His river of peace flowing through me. I know that all of my problems are dissolved in the Mind of God. God's ways are my ways. The words I have spoken accomplish that whereunto they are sent. I rejoice and give thanks, realizing that my prayers are answered. It is so.

At the end of two weeks I heard from her. "Your prayers worked wonders! I have been saying the prayers as you suggested, and I have been holding a picture of my husband in my mind. He got a job, and he is sober. He gets $120 weekly now. My doctor checked my blood pressure and it is normal, and all the blotches on my skin have cleared up. I don't have to take asthma medicine any more."

This woman's accumulated negative thoughts and mental pictures were the cause of her chronic worry. As she identified mentally and emotionally with the truths given her, they began to sink into her mind. She also painted pictures of health and vitality for herself and of achievement and accomplishment for her husband. These mental images were etched on her deeper mind, and her subconscious brought them all to fruition.

Worry Can Cause Diabetes

Dr. Flanders Dunbar comments as follows on the effects of worry in cases of diabetes: [7]

> In 1935 W. C. Menninger reported in two articles a study of the psychological factors in diabetes. He found that a few observers have given importance to psychic factors in the genesis of the disease. Opinions included: (1) the belief that 'diabetes may be caused by anxiety,' presented in 1891 by two psychiatrists, Maudsley and Savage; (2) psychic shock as an exciting cause; (3) 'worry, anxiety, and nervous strain are among the most frequent events in the diabetic anamnesis' (F. M. Allen, an internist); and (4) comments on 'remarkable coincidences' of emotional shock and the onset of diabetes. He says

---

[7] From *Emotions and Bodily Changes*, by Flanders Dunbar, M.D., Med.Sc.D., Ph.D. Fourth Edition, 1954, pp. 326–327. Permission granted by Columbia University Press, 2960 Broadway, New York 27, N.Y.

that to the internist the majority of cases do not present conspicuous psychopathology.

Menninger points out that all the quoted authors agreed that diabetes may be accelerated or aggravated by emotional states. He remarks: 'One is impressed with the inconsistency of the opinions that there is no denial of the great importance of the psychogenic factors once diabetes is established, and yet so conservative an opinion as to these same influences initiating the metabolic disorder.'

His own material includes thirty cases of diabetes and mental disorder. From study of this material Menninger found depression and anxiety to be the most common mental states associated with diabetes. He found no preponderance of type of mental disorder in diabetics, except that psychoneuroses of various types were frequent. Twelve of the twenty-two patients included in the first report showed paranoid delusions as an outstanding symptom. Five of these twenty-two patients demonstrated clearly to the author that diabetes may result from psychological disturbances. He states, however, that one must refer to multiple etiologic factors in attempting to explain the causes of diabetes. In conclusion, he says there is not much doubt that diabetes develops as a part of the expression of an individual's total personality conflict, and he feels justified in speaking of a 'diabetic personality reaction.' For fuller case histories of diabetics see Dunbar's *Psychosomatic Diagnosis* (3374a, 1943) and *Synopsis of Psychosomatic Diagnosis and Treatment* (3377, 1948).

His Worry Was Not Caused by His Problem

Once an executive came to me and told me that he was terribly worried that he would not get the presidency at his company's next scheduled board meeting. He added that he was next in line and this constant worry and anxiety were about to give him a nervous breakdown.

In talking to him I discovered that he had been worrying most of his life, and I remarked that he just *thought* his worry was due to the possibility that he would not be promoted. He did not agree with this. I told him to picture himself as president and to imagine that his associates were congratulating him on his promotion. He faithfully followed these instructions, and he was duly installed as president at the next board meeting.

About a month later, however, he again came to see me. He was still worrying, and his doctor had said that his blood pressure was dangerously high. I reminded him that he had previously attributed his worry to the fact that he might not be made president of his organization, but now that he was president he had not stopped worrying. He was worrying about the fact that he might not live up to the expectations of the executive board, that his decisions might cause the company to go in the red, and that he might be asked to resign.

He began to look inside himself, and suddenly he realized that his whole trouble was due to the fact that he did not make a habit of prayer and had no real contact with Infinite Power from which he could draw strength and security. He had thought that he was cursed with these worries; but now he awakened to the naked truth that he alone was their creator, and that by deciding to establish a prayer pattern he could overcome his obsession.

I gave him this suggestion: "When you waken in the morning use the following prayer:"

> I know that the answer to my problem lies in the God-Self within me. I now get quiet, still, and relaxed. I am at peace. I know God speaks in peace and not in confusion. I am now in tune with the Infinite; I know and believe implicitly that Infinite Intelligence is revealing to me the perfect answer. I think about the solution to my problems. I now live in the mood I would have were my problem solved. I truly live in this abiding faith and trust which is the mood of the solution; this is the spirit of God moving within me. This Spirit is Omnipotent; it is manifesting itself; my whole being rejoices in the solu-

tion; I am glad. I live in this feeling and I give thanks.

I know that God has the answer, for with God all things are possible. God is the Living Spirit Almighty within me; He is the Source of all wisdom and illumination.

The indicator of the presence of God within me is a sense of peace and poise. I now cease all sense of strain and struggle; I trust the God-Power implicitly. I know that all the wisdom and power I need to live a glorious and successful life are within me. I relax my entire body; my faith is in His wisdom; I go free. I claim and feel the peace of God flooding my mind, my heart, and my whole being. I know that the quiet mind gets its problems solved. I now turn my request over to the God-Presence, knowing It has an answer. I am at peace.

He repeated the above prayer three times each morning, knowing that through repetition these truths would sink into his subconscious and establish a healing, wholesome habit of constructive thinking. He also realized that he now was anchored to the God-Power within him in which he lived, moved, and had his being. His sense of union with God gave him confidence to overcome anything about which he had mistakenly worried. Through this shift in his mental attitude, he became a balanced man.

How She Got Off the Merry-Go-Round

A woman once visited me and said that she was worried about her boy in school. She feared that he might get the measles, fall into a swimming pool, or be run over by a truck. She really was on a worry debauch. She said to me, "I must worry. I can't stop worrying."

I told her that it would be much more interesting, fascinating, absorbing, and thrilling to bless her boy rather than to throw mental bricks at him all day long. I suggested that she open her mind, let in the Higher Power, and realize that God loves her boy, that He watches over him, that His Overshadowing Presence protects the boy at all times, and that God's love surrounds him, enfolds him, and enwraps him.

As she practiced blessing her boy, she cast out all her gloom of worry and misery. She made a habit of prayer—and prayer is a habit.

This woman's worry, fretfulness, and morbid thoughts about her son were due to laziness and indifference in allowing these destructive pictures to influence her thoughts and emotions. You can heal yourself as did this woman by following the injunction of the Psalmist: *"I will lift up mine eyes unto the hills, from whence cometh my help."* (Psalm 121:1) Do this regularly and you will be released from the vexation of worry.

You Don't Want It

When you worry, you are focusing your attention and directing your mind on that which you don't want, so that you create conditions, experiences, and events which disturb you. Worry means that you are using your mind negatively and destructively.

How Worry Affects All Glands and Organs of Our Body

Dr. Hans Sclye, at the University of Montreal's Institute of Experimental Medicine and Surgery, demonstrated the destructive effects of worry, fear, and anxiety on the general defence system of the body: [8]

---

[8] From *The Mind in Healing*, by Rolf Alexander, M.D., page 14, published 1960. Permission granted by E. P. Dutton & Co., Inc., 201 Park Avenue South, New York 3, N.Y.

If the mental stress which set [the general defence system] in motion is not of a temporary and passing nature, but persists week after week, the adrenal glands first attempt to adapt to the situation by increasing their output of hormones, but this plays havoc with various other processes not related to defence. The individual may develop arthritis or diabetes, or any of the other so-called psychosomatic diseases. Inevitably if the stress is continued beyond this "general adaptation" stage, the adrenals become exhausted. They change in colour from yellow to brown, the stomach becomes spotted with ulcers; the resistance to cold and heat and to every kind of disease and injury collapses, and if the unfortunate individual does not fall victim to some infection he will probably succumb to one of the heart, circulatory or kidney diseases, which are today our greatest killers.

Dr. Selye's work demonstrated that the defence system can effectively fight only one thing at a time. If in response to a mental tension caused by pain from a broken limb, for instance. it is set into action, it quickly organizes a hundred specialized activities, in addition to its general work, to repair the fracture. But if in the middle of this repair work another stress, caused by fear let us say, is introduced, we either quickly succumb to the first injury, or to "shock" resulting from the second stress— or the broken limb simply does not mend and has to be amputated. In the case of other diseases rather than fractures, healing is suspended and the diseases become "chronic." Thus, if our general defence system is mobilized by mental tensions of a non-physical origin, our resistance to the extra stresses imposed by such things as pneumonia, influenza, colds, is decreased proportionally.

He Raised His Sights

A young intern consistently worried about his future; he was a nervous wreck. However, he learned to paint a picture of himself as filling a staff position in a big hospital and possessing a sumptuous office in the city. In his imagery he had a liveried chauffeur, and he imagined that friends constantly were congratulating him.

He kept this mental picture before him; it was his mental movie. He attended to it and devoted himself to this picture, and whenever he was prone to worry, he purposefully flashed the picture on the screen of his mind. As the weeks passed by, a higher power moved on his behalf, honoring his dreams and making them all real. The chief surgeon invited him to be his assistant, and he married a very wealthy woman who purchased for him a most sumptuous office and furthermore also provided him with a Cadillac and a liveried chauffeur.

This is the way by which the habit of worry is changed. This is the way the old man becomes a new man in God. *"Cast thy burden upon the Lord, and he shall sustain thee . . ."* (Psalm 55:22)

You Can Overcome Worry

Do not spend time looking at your troubles or problems; cease all negative thinking. Your mind cannot function harmoniously when it is tense. It relieves the strain to do something soothing and pleasant when you are presented with a problem. You do not fight a problem—you *can* overcome it.

To release pressure, take a drive; go for a walk; play solitaire; or read a favorite chapter of the Bible, such as the Eleventh Chapter of Hebrews or Chapter Thirteen of I Corinthians. Or, read the Forty-Sixth Psalm; read it over carefully and quietly several times. An inner calm will steal over you, and you will become poised and peaceful.

Steps in Prayer for Overcoming Worry

The First Step: Every morning when you awaken, turn to God in prayer and know that God is your loving Father. Relax your body; then have a dialogue with God, which is your Higher Self. Become as a little child; this means that you trust the God-Presence completely and you know that God is healing you now.

The Second Step: Affirm lovingly: "Thank you, Father, for this wonderful day. It is God's day; it is filled with joy, peace, happiness, and success for me. I look forward with a happy expectancy to this day. The wisdom and inspiration of God will govern me during the entire day. God is my partner; everything I do will turn out in a wonderful way. I believe that God is guiding me, and His love fills my soul."

The Third Step: Claim boldly: "I am full of confidence in the goodness of God. I know that He watches over me at all times. I let go; I am poised, serene, and calm. I know that it is God in action in all phases of my life, and Divine law and order reign supreme."

Make a habit of dwelling on these three steps to prayer, and when worry thoughts come to your mind, substitute any of the spiritual thoughts from the above three steps; gradually, your mind will be conditioned to peace.

POWER-POINTERS

1. When you worry, you brood over a great many things that never will happen, and you deplete yourself of vitality, enthusiasm, and energy.
2. When you worry, you are anxious about that which has not happened but that which may happen. Change your present mode of thought and you will change your future. *Your future is your present thought made manifest.*
3. If you sustain the worry habit, you may attract what you are worrying about.
4. When morbid, negative thoughts come to your mind, supplant them by affirming: "God is with me." This destroys the negative thought which is only a vibration.
5. If you are worried about a husband or anybody else, mentally picture him as you would wish to see him. Frequent habitation of your mind with this picture will work miracles.
6. The chronic worrier is not worried about that problem which he says he is worried about. The basic reason is a deep sense of insecurity, because he has not joined himself with God.
7. Don't worry about your boy or girl in school. Realize the Presence of God where your child is, and mentally envelop the child with God's love, peace, and joy. Know that the whole armor of God enfolds your

child, and that he will always be protected from all harm.

8. When you worry, you really are praying for what you don't want.

9. Unite with a Higher Power and let the Almighty move through your new constructive pattern of thought and imagery, and the Light of God will dispel all gloom, worry, and despair. Let in the sunshine of His love.

The

Replenishing Law
of automatic prosperity

People are constantly asking, "How can I get ahead in life, improve my circumstances, get a raise in salary, buy a new car and a new home, and have all the money I need in order to do what I have to do when I want to do it?"

The answer to all of these questions comes through learning to use the laws of your own mind: the law of cause and effect, the law of increase, and the law of attraction; these laws of your mind work with the same precision and exactitude as do the laws of physics, chemistry, and mathematics—and as definitely as the law of gravitation. The law of prosperity is beautifully expressed by the Psalmist when he says, "*His delight is in the law*

of the Lord; and in his law doth he meditate day and night."
(Psalm 1:2)

Prosperity means to increase our capacities and abilities along all lines and in every direction so that we release our inner powers. The promotion, the money, and the contacts you wish to make are the images or likenesses, as well as the physical forms of the states of mind which produce them.

How a Broker Prospered

I am very well acquainted with a stock broker in Los Angeles. He attributes his large clientele and success in making money for them to his practice of a mental, imaginary conversation with a multimillionaire banker friend who congratulates him on his wise and sound judgment and who compliments him on his purchase of the right stocks. He dramatizes this imaginary conversation every morning before he goes to his office, and he psychologically fixes the impression on his subconscious.

This broker's imaginary conversations agree with his aim to make sound investments for himself and his clients. He told me that his main purpose in his business life is to make money for others and to see them prosper financially by his wise counsel. In making money for others, he also has prospered beyond his fondest dreams. It is quite evident that he is using the laws of mind constructively and that his delight is in the law of the Lord.

His Subconscious Paid His Mortgage

Once a man said to me, "I will lose everything—my home, car, and land. I can't meet the note at my bank, and they are going to foreclose on me." I explained to him that if he would use his subconscious mind in the right way, it would provide him with the needed money. He was not to wonder how, when, or where. He was not to think of what source. The subconscious has ways you know not of; its ways are past finding out.

At my suggestion, prior to sleep at night he began to imagine himself depositing the required currency at his bank, i.e., giving it to the cashier and hearing the cashier say to him, "You are all paid up. I'm glad you obtained the money!" He became intensely interested in his mental picture, or imaginary act; he made it seem real and natural. The more earnestly he engaged his mind in the imaginary drama, the more effectively was the imaginary act deposited in the bank of his subconscious. He made it so real and true that it had to take place physically.

The sequel to this was interesting. This man one night had a vivid dream of a horse coming in in first place—a real longshot, 50 to 1—at the Hollywood Race Track. He also dreamed that the cashier at the race track said to him, "Ten thousand dollars for you; boy, you're lucky!" He suddenly arose and awakened his wife to tell her of his dream. She said to him, "There are two one hundred-dollar bills that I put in an old teapot five years ago for a rainy day; now, those bills will rain blessings from Heaven for us. Go to the track and put them on the nose!"

His horse came in at 50 to 1, just as he had seen in his dream, and, as the race track cashier was paying him off, he said the exact words he had heard in his dream. He went to the bank and paid the $10,000 note in currency, as he had previously subjectively dramatized so vividly and earnestly.

"*. . . I the Lord will make myself known unto him in a vision, and will speak unto him in a dream.*" (Numbers 12:6)

The Magic of Increase

A woman wrote to me some time ago and said, "Bills are piling up; I am out of work. I have three children and no money. What shall I do?"

At my suggestion she began to give thanks for God's bountiful supply. Several times a day she relaxed her body in an arm chair and entered into a drowsy, sleepy state, or a state akin to sleep. She condensed the ideas of her needs into these wonderful magic-working words of increase: "God multiplies my good exceedingly." She understood that whatever she gave attention to, her subsconscious would magnify and multiply a hundred-fold. The significance of these words to her meant the realization of all of her desires, such as all bills paid, a new position, a home, a husband, food and clothing for her children, and an ample supply of money.

During her periods of prayer, she did not permit her mind to wander; she focused and concentrated her attention on the meaning of the words, "God multiplies my good exceedingly." She repeated this phrase over and over again until it had the feeling of reality.

The idea of using a simple phrase as in the above example is based upon a knowledge of the laws of mind. When you restrict your attention to one simple phrase, your mind is prevented from wandering. Ideas are conveyed to the subconscious by repetition, faith, and expectancy.

This woman had astounding results. Her brother came home from New Zealand unannounced; she had not seen or heard from him in twenty years. He not only gave her $15,000 in cash but some valuable diamonds as gifts. At her brother's suggestion, she became a secretary to a lawyer; she married her boss within a month! She paid off all her debts, and she informed me that she is supremely happy.

The ways of the subconscious truly are past finding out. Your subconscious multiplies 30-fold, 60-fold, and 100-fold. This is the magic of increase.

"Thank You" Opens the Way to Prosperity

It is amazing how the thankful attitude improves every department of your life, including your health and happiness as well as your prosperity.

A real estate broker proved this in a wonderful way. He had been having a great deal of difficulty in selling homes and properties which were listed with him, and he was frustrated and unhappy. Convinced of the prosperity-power of the grateful heart, however, he began to pray every night, affirming as follows: "Father, I thank thee that thou hast heard me, and I know that thou hearest me always." [9] Then, just prior to sleep, he condensed the phrase to two words: "Thank you." He repeated them over and over again, as a lullaby; he continued to speak these two words silently until he fell asleep.

One night, in a dream, he saw a man who gave him a check for fourteen lots and a home which he particularly desired to sell. In a week's time, the man whom he had seen in his dream came into his real estate office and bought the property which he had previously foreseen in his dream.

This real estate broker has made a habit of feelingly repeating every night the words, "Thank you," until he falls off into the deep of sleep. His health has remarkably improved, his wealth is soaring, and, quite frequently in his dream life, he has a preview of the sale of certain properties which subsequently is verified objectively in all details.

As this man does, silently decree morning and night that God is prospering you in mind, body, and affairs; feel the reality of

---

[9] See John 11:41–42.

it, and you will never want for anything. Repeat over and over again as a lullaby, "Thank you, Father," as you prepare for sleep; this means that you are thanking your Higher Self for abundance, health, wealth, and harmony. It may also happen that the Lord (your subconscious mind) may answer you in a vision and speak to you in a dream.

She Decreed Prosperity

A woman wrote to me, saying, "I owe the bank a lot of money on my home, and bills are piling up." I replied to her, saying that she should decree with feeling several times a day, "My house is free from all debt, and wealth flows to me in avalanches of abundance." I pointed out that she was not to question the manner in which the answer to her prayer would come and that her subconscious intelligence would direct all her steps, for it knows everything necessary for the fulfillment of her desires.

A few weeks later, she was approached by a builder who wanted to put up an apartment house on her property, and he offered her far more than her property was worth. She accepted gratefully and was able to liquidate all of her debts. At the same time she secured a contract from the builder to act as manager of the apartment for him at a good salary and with a fine apartment.

Your subconscious always magnifies. The Bible says, "*Thou shalt also decree a thing, and it shall be established unto thee . . .*" (Job 22:28)

Life Is Addition

A business friend of mine, a tailor by trade, has a favorite saying: "All I ever do is add. I never subtract." He means that prosperity is a plus sign. *Add* to your growth, wealth, power, knowledge, faith, and wisdom.

He adds to his life by meditating on success, harmony, guidance, right action, and the law of opulence. He imagines and feels himself successful and prosperous, and his subconscious mind responds to his habitual thinking.

He Began to Sell Again

An insurance salesman once said to me, "I try so hard, and I work long hours, but my results are meagre and most disappointing." I arranged for him to have a session with me once a week. At these sessions I had him still his mind, relax, and let go; then I would pray for him as follows: "You are relaxed and at ease, poised, serene, and calm. By day and by night you are prospering spiritually, mentally, and financially. You are a tremendous success. You are open and receptive to new ideas. Your good is flowing to you freely, joyously, endlessly, and ceaselessly. The law of increase is working for you now."

Then he would pray for about five minutes in the same manner after my prayer, affirming these truths in the first person, present tense. These weekly get-togethers brought marvelous results. Within a few weeks he began to make new contacts, and his sales increased by leaps and bounds. He discovered that a changed attitude changed everything in his life.

His Subconscious Made Him a Millionaire

I shall now proceed to show you how you may definitely and positively convey an idea or mental image to your subconscious mind.

Your conscious mind is personal and selective. It chooses,

selects, weighs, analyzes, dissects, and investigates. It is capable of inductive and deductive reasoning. The subjective, or subconscious, mind is subject to the conscious mind. It might be called a servant of the conscious mind. The subconscious obeys the order of the conscious mind. Focused, directed thoughts reach the subjective level; they must be of a certain degree of intensity. Intensity is acquired by concentration.

A man who owned a hamburger stand in the Middle West wrote me and said that he had read *The Power of Your Subconscious Mind* when it first came on the market. He wrote that he had decided to concentrate on a million dollars, as he wished to expand his business and have several restaurants; he also wanted to establish a branch in his native country in Europe.

He followed the technique of impregnating his subconscious mind by concentrating on a million dollars. To concentrate is to come back to the center and to contemplate the infinite riches of the subconscious mind. Every night he stilled the activity of his mind and entered into a quiet, relaxed, mental state. He gathered all his thoughts together and focused all his attention on a million dollar deposit in his bankbook. He gave all his attention to this mental image. His steadied attention made a deep, lasting impression on the sensitive plate of his subconscious mind.

He repeated this drama every night, and at the end of one month things began to happen. He married a very wealthy woman who loved his ambition, zeal, enthusiasm, and dreams for accomplishment. She bought a restaurant for him which, within a few months' time, proved to be a tremendous success; he has opened two branches. He has made some investments in oil stock which is pyramiding fantastically. He sent me a gift of five hundred dollars for having written the book, which was one of the most delightful presents I have ever received.

This man has over a million dollars in the bank at the time of this writing, and, in addition, his subconscious has furnished him extra dividends, including a beautiful and fabulously wealthy wife, a newborn baby, and a life more abundant.

Prayer for Prosperity

"*. . . Thou shalt make thy way prosperous, and then thou shalt have good success.*" (Joshua 1:8) I now give a pattern of success and prosperity to the deeper mind within me, which is the law. I now identify myself with the Infinite Source of supply. I listen to the still, small voice of God within me. This inner voice leads, guides, and governs all my activities. I am one with the abundance of God. I know and believe that there are new and better ways of conducting my business; Infinite Intelligence reveals the new ways to me.

I am growing in wisdom and understanding. My business is God's business. I am Divinely prospered in all ways. Divine Wisdom within me reveals the ways and means by which all my affairs are adjusted in the right way immediately.

The words of faith and conviction which I now speak open up all the necessary doors or avenues for my success and prosperity. I know that "*the Lord (Law) will perfect that which concerneth me . . .*" (Psalm 138:8) My feet are kept in the perfect path, because I am a son of the living God.

SOME PROFITABLE POINTERS

1. Learn to use the laws of your mind, and you can attract to yourself wealth, love, happiness, and the life more abundant.

2. Decide to make money for others, and you also will make it for yourself; you will prosper beyond your fondest dreams.

3. Your subconscious mind has ways you know not of. Give it the idea of prosperity, and it will do the rest.

4. A wonderful prosperity formula is to affirm frequently and feelingly: "God multiplies my good exceedingly." Wonders happen as you pray in this way.

5. The thankful heart always is close to God. Use the Bible prayer; it is marvelous: *"Father, I thank thee that thou hast heard me, and I knew that thou hearest me always."* (John 11:41–42) Lull yourself to sleep with "thank you" on your lips.

6. You can decree a thing, and it shall come to pass, such as: "My home is free from all debt, and wealth flows to me in avalanches of abundance." Be sincere and mean it, and your subconscious will respond.

7. Life is addition. Add to your wealth, power, wisdom, knowledge, and faith by studying the law of your conscious and subconscious mind.

8. Affirm, "My good is flowing to me now, ceaselessly, tirelessly, joyously, and copiously," and God's riches will flow into your receptive, open mind.

9. You can convey to your subconscious mind the idea

of a million dollars through concentration and focused attention, and in due season your subconscious will answer you in its own way. One prerequisite is sincerity and undivided attention.

10. "*. . . Thou shalt make thy way prosperous, and then thou shalt have good success.*" (Joshua 1:8)

The
$\mathfrak{P}$enultimate $\mathfrak{L}$aw
of creation

Napoleon said, "Imagination rules the world." Henry Ward Beecher said, "The mind without imagination is what an observatory would be without a telescope." Pascal said, "Imagination disposes of everything; it creates beauty, justice, happiness, which are everything in this world."

The faculty of image-making is called imagination. It is one of the primal faculties of mind and has the power to project and clothe your ideas, giving them visibility on the screen of space. You can discipline, control, and direct your imagination constructively and get what you want in life, or you can use it negatively and imagine what you don't want in life. The mental images which you contemplate and consciously accept as true are impressed on your subconscious mind and made manifest in your life.

Imagination is the mighty instrument used by famous scientists, artists, poets, physicists, inventors, architects, and mystics. When the world says, "It is impossible, it can't be done," the man with vivid imagination says, "It *is* done!"

How He Became President

Mr. Fred Reinecke, President of Febco Corporation, Glendale, California, brought to my attention the success power of his imagination. The following is from his letter, which he has given me permission to publish:

> I entered business with my brothers and sisters in 1949. Our business burned to the ground three months later. We refused to go into bankruptcy or cry over spilt milk. We decided to rebuild, and I kept picturing in my mind a large corporation with salesmen all over the country. I pictured in my mind a great building, factory, offices, good facilities, knowing that through the alchemy of mind I could weave the fabric out of which my dreams would be clothed. You were of tremendous help to me, and you gave me a great lift on the occasion of my first visit to you when you called me "Mr. President." You began to introduce me to others at church as "president of a multi-million-dollar corporation." Mentally, I had not quite accepted the title of president; it seemed an utter impossibility, as my brother was president. I began to think it over, and after a few weeks I accepted the title, "President," and affirmed, "I am president of my corporation in Divine order. Either this or something grander or greater in the sight of Infinite Intelligence." I pictured a sumptuous office with my name on the door and the title, President's Office. I accepted it completely with a smile. It looked good to me!
>
> Then things began to happen. First, my brother, who was vice president, decided to leave; several months later my other brother, the president of the corporation, an-

nounced that he was leaving to run for Congress of the United States. My sister also left and attained a higher position in life. All members of my family are happy in their new undertakings, and I constantly pray for their guidance and true place in the same way as I pray for myself.

Now, suddenly, I *was* President! This enormous step which had seemed an impossibility only eighteen months before had become a reality, and today the business is flourishing beyond my fondest dreams. I believe implicitly what you teach—that "Imagination is the workshop of God."

Her Creative Imagination Healed Her

Dr. Olive Gaze of Brentwood, California, has tremendous faith and believes and understands the magical power of creative imagination. She is a lineal descendant of the world-famous preacher, Henry Ward Beecher. Dr. Gaze submitted the following letter on the power of constructive imagination:

Dear Mr. Murphy: I was driving my late husband, Dr. Harry Gaze, and as we turned onto Sunset Boulevard, suddenly a frightful crash spun our car around; we both were rendered unconscious. When I came to, policemen were standing around us, and Harry was carried off in an ambulance. In my dazed state, I gave the policeman my doctor's home address and telephone number and your address and telephone number, which I never had memorized in my conscious mind. It was my subconscious speaking and acting. A most amazing thing is that I gave the policeman the name and exact address and telephone number of my maid, who was spending the weekend with her daughter in Woodland Hills; consciously, I did not know their address and had no idea of the phone number. This indicates true clairvoyance and is a perfect example of how the subconscious takes over.

I found myself in the hospital. My pelvis had been broken in several places, and I heard that I would not walk again. I began to imagine myself walking in to your lectures, and I pictured you shaking hands with me and congratulating me, saying, "You look wonderful! It is the miracle-working power of God."

I had absolute faith in the healing power of God, and while I was in the hospital I constantly pictured myself as doing all the things I ordinarily would do were I to be made whole. I kept affirming constantly, "God is healing me now. God made all the bones of my body, and they are all in their true place, ministering to me."

What I felt and imagined to be true, came to pass. I now know that the creative power of God flows through our mental images. It is wonderful!

Her Imagination Healed Herself and Her Family

The following letter from Mrs. Fred Reinecke of Glendale, California, is published with her permission:

Dear Dr. Murphy: In a deep state of depression I found myself locked up in the Camarillo State Mental Hospital. During clinical therapy, I met myself face to face; I learned to know myself and how to adjust to myself and others. I constantly affirmed, "God's love fills my soul, and He guides me." I got over the acute depression and was released.

I feel that God guided me to hear you lecture on the power of our subconscious mind. You stressed the amazing and miraculous power of mental imagery.

I began mentally to picture myself as happy, joyous, free, and prosperous. I mentally pictured a beautiful home, and many times a day I would sit down and picture my husband as a tremendous success, prosperous, and Divinely happy. I would imagine that he was telling me how happy he was, how much he loved me, and how successful his business was. I pictured my daughter and son as they ought to be: brilliant students, industrious, and full of zeal and enthusiasm.

I steadily built the mental picture of a peaceful, happy, and joyous life; I lived with it daily. Per your instructions, every night I imagined that you were congratulating me on my inner peace, tranquility, happiness, and freedom. I could see you smile, and I heard the tonal quality of your voice. I made it real and vivid, and all that I mentally have pictured for myself, my husband, and my two children, has come to pass.

Imagining Produces a Great Teacher

While visiting the Round Towers of Ireland, I met a teacher who seemed to be in a very pensive mood. I asked him, "On what are you meditating?" This is the essence of his answer:

He pointed out that it is only by dwelling on the great and wonderful ideas of the world that we grow and expand. He contemplated the age of the stones in the Towers; then his imagination took him back to the quarries where the stones first were formed. His imagination "unclothed" the stones. He saw with his internal eye the structure, geological formation, and composition of the stones reduced to the formless state; finally, he imagined the oneness of the stones with all stones and all life. He realized in his Divine imagery that it was possible to reconstruct the history of the Irish race from looking at the Round Towers!

Through his imaginative faculty, this teacher was able to see imaginary, invisible men living in the Tower and to hear their voices. The whole place became alive to him in his imagination. Through this power, he was able to go back in time to where there were no Round Towers. In his mind, he began to weave a drama of the place from which stones originated, who brought them, the purpose of the structure, and the history connected with it. He said to me, "I am able almost to feel the touch and hear the sound of steps that vanished thousands of years ago."

This teacher was immensely popular, and he told me that his writings and lectures brought him vast sums of money, all of which he said were due to his practice of the faculty of imagination.

Science and Imagination

It is from the realm of imagination that have come television, radio, radar, superjets, and all other modern inventions. Your imagination is the treasure house of infinity, which releases from your subconscious mind all the precious jewels of music, art, poetry, and invention. You can look at some ancient ruin, an old temple, or a pyramid, and you can reconstruct the records of the dead past. In the ruins of an old church yard, you also can see a modern city, resurrected in all its former beauty and glory.

You may be in the prison of want and lack, or behind stone bars, but in your imagination you can find an undreamed of measure of freedom.

Great Accomplishments Through Imagining

Chico, the Parisian sewer cleaner, imagined and lived in a paradisaical mental state called "the seventh heaven," even though he never saw the light of day.

Bunyan, in prison, wrote the great masterpiece, *Pilgrim's Progress.* He used his imaginative faculty to create such characters as Christian, Evangelist, Faithful, Hopeful, and Giant Despair, which represent characteristics, qualities, and patterns of behavior in all of us. These were all fictitious characters, but as moods, feelings, beliefs, attitudes, and capacities of human nature, they will live forever in the hearts of men.

Milton, though blind, saw with his interior eye. His imagination made his brain a ball of fire, and he wrote *Paradise Lost.* In this way, he brought some of God's Paradise to all men everywhere. Imagination was Milton's spiritual eye; imagination enabled him to go about God's business, whereby he annihilated time, space, and matter and brought forth the truths of the Invisible Presence.

Imagining Brought Her Money and Recognition

Some years ago, a young lady, deeply religious and a graduate of the University of California at Los Angeles, said to me, "I want to write short stories and fiction, but all my articles are returned to me. I'm getting a rejection complex."

I advised her to create a story in her mind which would teach something about the golden rule, to pass that story and all of its characters through her spiritual and highly artistic mentality, and to claim and know that her writing would be fascinating, intensely interesting, and instructive to the public. I suggested that, prior to sleep every night, she imagine that I was congratulating her on her success and the acceptance of her article, and that her visual imagery would sink into her subconscious mind. I also told her that as she persevered, results would follow.

The sequel to her new attitude of mind and mental imagery is intensely interesting. Two magazines accepted her articles, and a psychologist paid her $2,000 to edit and re-write his book for him. As this book goes to press, she is writing a novel, and the outline has been accepted by a publisher.

Imagination Brought Him Success

In Greenwich Village, New York, I was acquainted with a poet who wrote beautiful verses; he had them printed on cards and sold them at Christmas time.

Some of his poems were beautiful gems of spiritual love. He said that when he would get still, the words would come into his mind accompanied by a lovely scene. Flowers, people, and his friends would come clearly into his mind. He said that these images spoke to him; they told him their story. Often, the poem, song, or lullaby would appear complete and ready in his mind without the slightest effort.

His habit was to imagine that he was writing beautiful poems which would stir the hearts of men. He was immensely successful in the sale of these cards, and he reaped a small fortune.

Imagining Promoted a Chemist

I had a conversation some years ago with a young chemist, who stated that for years his superiors had tried to manufacture a certain German dye, but had failed. He had been given the assignment when he first was employed by them. He commented that he had not known it could not be done, and that he had synthesized the compound without any difficulty.

His superiors had been amazed and wanted to know his secret. His answer was that he imagined that he had the answer. Pressed further by his superiors, he had said that he could clearly see the letters, "Answer," in blazing red color in his mind; then he created a vacuum underneath the letters, knowing that as he imagined the chemical formula underneath the letters, his subconscious would fill it in. The third night, he had had a dream in which the complete formula and the technique for making the compound were clearly presented. This had resulted in a wonderful promotion to an executive capacity in the organization for this young chemist.

Imagination Discovered America

All of us have read the story of Columbus and his discovery of America. It was imagination that led him to his discovery. His imagination plus faith in a Divine power led him on and brought him to victory. The sailors said to Columbus, "What shall we do when all hope is gone?" His reply was, "You shall say at break of day, 'Sail on, sail on, sail on and on.'"

Here is the key to prayer: be faithful to the end, full of faith every step of the way, persisting to the end, and knowing in your heart that the end is secure because you saw the end. Having seen and felt the end, you have willed the means to the realization of the end.

How Imagination Makes the Past Alive

Archaeologists and paleontologists studying the tombs of ancient Egypt, through their imaginative perception, reconstruct ancient scenes. The dead past becomes alive and audible once more.

Looking at the ancient ruins and the hieroglyphics thereon, the scientist's imagination enables him to clothe the ancient temple with roofs and to surround them with gardens, pools, and fountains. The fossil remains are clothed with eyes, sinews, and muscles, and they again walk and talk.

The past becomes the living present, and we find that in imagination there is no time or space. Through your imaginative faculty, you can be a companion of the most inspired writers of all time.

A Widow Re-Marries Through Imagining

A lonely widow decided to use her imaginative faculty for an ideal husband and a perfect marriage. With her power of imagination, she saw me as the minister officiating at her elaborate wedding. In her imagination, she heard me pronounce the words; she saw the flowers and the church, and she heard the music. She felt the imaginary ring on her finger; its solidity and tangibility were natural to her. She traveled, through her imagination, on her honeymoon to Niagara Falls and on to Europe.

A few weeks later, she was invited to San Francisco as a guest of her daughter and her daughter's husband; she accepted the invitation. Her son-in-law held a reception in his home as a welcoming gesture to his mother-in-law. There, she was introduced by her son-in-law to a wealthy realtor, a long-time friend of his whose wife recently had passed on.

This introduction deepened into a romance, and within three months they were married by the author. They then left on a honeymoon to Niagara Falls and Europe, just as she had been subjectively imagining. She wrote me from Paris, France, saying, "Everything that I had imagined and had felt as true has come to pass in such a unique and extraordinary manner that I am deeply moved when I contemplate the powers of my mind."

Graduates with Honors Through Imagining

A high school girl once was told by her mother that she could not attend a certain college because she had to go to work as there was not enough money to support the family of four. Her mother was a widow and the main support of their family. This young girl came on Sunday morning to hear a series of lectures on *The Power of Your Subconscious Mind*.

She began to practice what she had heard, which was that her imagination could and would clothe all her ideas in form. Several times a day she mentally created a beautiful scenic drama. She imagined the president of the college giving her a diploma; she pictured all the students dressed in gowns. She heard her mother congratulating her; she felt her mother's embrace and her kiss. She made it all real, natural, dramatic, exciting, and wonderful. She said to herself, "There is a creative intelligence in my subconscious mind with power to mold all these forms which I am picturing in my mind and to endow them with life, motion, and reality."

A few months passed by, and suddenly and unexpectedly out of the blue, her wealthy aunt in New York sent her $3,000 as a gift for her eighteenth birthday—the check was marked "Gift from Auntie." She wrote a thank-you note to her aunt, saying how grateful she was and that her mother had said to her, "You can go to college now; we'll manage somehow." Her aunt wrote back and requested that all her college bills be sent to her for full payment!

This girl's subconscious mind had given her more than compound interest. She said to me, "My good came to me, pressed down, shaken together, and running over!" She graduated magna cum laude. This is an example of the miracle-working powers of your imagination.

A Boy Healed His Mother Through Imagining

Once I interviewed a very religious school boy about fourteen years old. He told me that whenever he had a problem, he would imagine that Jesus was talking to him, giving him the answer to his problem and telling him what to do.

This boy's mother was very ill, and frequently the boy would get still and quiet and imagine that Jesus was saying to him, "Go thy way; your mother is made whole!" He made that drama of his mind so real, vivid, and intense that, due to his faith and belief, he convinced himself of the truth of what he subjectively heard. His mother *was* completely healed; yet she had been considered as hopeless and beyond medical help.

The boy had galvanized himself into the feeling of being one with his image, and according to his faith or conviction was it done unto him. As the boy changed his mental attitude about his mother and imagined her perfect health, the idea of perfect health was simultaneously resurrected in his subconscious mind. There is but one healing power, namely, your subconscious mind. He had operated the law unconsciously, and he had believed in his own mind that Jesus actually was talking to him; then according to his belief his subconscious responded.

This is why Paracelsus said in the sixteenth century, "Whether the object of your belief be true or false, you will get the same results."

Imagination, the Workshop of God

"*Where there is no vision, the people perish . . .*" (Proverbs 29:18) My vision is that I desire to know more of God and the way He works. My vision is for perfect health, harmony, and peace. My vision is the inner faith that Infinite Spirit heals and guides me now in all my ways. I know and believe that the God-Power within me answers my prayer; this is a deep conviction within me. I know that imagination is the result of what I image in my mind. Faith is, as Paul says, the substance out of which the image is formed. (Hebrews 11:1)

I make it my daily practice to imagine only for myself and for others also that which is noble, wonderful, and God-like. I now imagine that I am doing the thing I long to do; I imagine that I now possess the things I long to possess; I imagine that I am what I long to be. To make it real, I feel the reality of it, and I know that it is so. Thank you, Father.

USING YOUR IMAGINATION

1. The faculty of image-making is called "imagination." Imagination clothes all ideas and projects them on the screen of space.

2. You can picture a beautiful home, a trip, or a marriage, and, as you feel its reality, your mental image will be objectified.

3. Imagine yourself doing what you love to do and feel yourself in the act, and wonders will happen in your life.

4. Mentally picture yourself as whole and perfect, living in a beautiful home, with a successful husband or wife, and with a happy, joyous family. Persevere in this mental image, and miracles will happen in your life.

5. Through disciplined imagination, you can see with your interior eye the structure of ancient ruins, and, in your vivid imagination, you can reconstruct them and make the dead past seem to be alive.

6. It is the realm of imagination from which came television, radar, radio, super-jets, and all other modern inventions.

7. Writers use the imaginative faculty to create the great works which have immortalized great men as Shakespeare, Bunyan, Milton, and others.

8. Imagine that your writings will be fascinating and intensely interesting to the public, and imagine that you are being congratulated on your success. This

habitual imagery will sink into your subconscious mind and eventually come to pass.

9. Through the practice of imagining a beautiful poem, song, or play that you have written, often the poem, song, or the theme of the play will appear complete and ready in your mind without the slightest effort.

10. A chemist can imagine that he has the answer to a complex problem by contemplating the answer. Often, the answer will come in a dream—which is subconscious imagery—and the formula appears.

11. Looking at ancient ruins and the hieroglyphics thereon, the scientist's imagination enables him to clothe ancient temples with roofs and to surround them with gardens, pools, and fountains.

12. You can attract the right marriage partner by imagining your favorite minister saying, "I now pronounce you man and wife." Imagine and feel the ring on your finger as you go to sleep—you will be amazed at how quickly the subconscious answers you.

13. You can create mentally a beautiful scenic drama that you wish would come to pass. Make it vivid, real, natural, dramatic, and exciting. Your subconscious mind will accept what you imagine and feel, and it will bring it to pass.

14. You can imagine that a loved one is telling you that he or she has had a miraculous healing. Rejoice in it, and see your loved one as vital and strong. Picture your loved one smiling, hear the good news, and feel the embrace, and you will galvanize yourself into the feeling of being one with your image. Your prayer will be answered!

The
Ultimate Law
of infinite life

The Omnipresence of God means that God, or Infinite Life, is present everywhere at every moment of time and point of space. To practice the Presence of God all day long is the key to harmony, health, peace, joy, and the fullness of life. The practice of the Presence is powerful beyond imagination. Do not overlook it because of its utter simplicity.

You must realize that all creation is the expression of God in infinite differentiation. You are an individualized expression of God or Life, and God is forever seeking to express through you at higher and higher levels. Consequently you are here to glorify God and to enjoy Him forever.

Begin now to contemplate the greatest of all truths, the all-inclusive and all-encompassing truth that God is the only cause, power, and substance in the world and that everything you see, feel, and touch is a part of His Self-expression.

How to Begin

I am acquainted with many people who sit down for five or ten minutes every day and meditate on the fact that God is absolute bliss, peace, harmony, joy, infinite intelligence, Who is all-powerful, and Who radiates boundless wisdom and infinite love. They let their thoughts dwell on these truths; they look at these qualities and powers of God from all angles; then they begin to be aware that every person they meet is an expression of God; and that, in fact, everything they see is God made manifest; it is God dramatizing Himself for the joy of expressing Himself. As they do this, they find their whole world changing; they consistently experience better health, outer conditions improve, and they are possessed of a new vitality and energy.

He Found His Son After Seven Years

Mr. Michael Sands of Los Angeles, who attends my lecturers and handles the distribution of my recordings, told me about an amazing episode in his life. About seven years ago, he had to leave a South American country, and he left a message for his son to follow him. His son never received the message. The boy tried to get in touch with his mother, who was separated from his father, but she also had moved and had left no forwarding address. The many letters and cables sent by Mr. Sands to his son and his business acquaintances in South America proved to be of no avail. All known agencies could not locate his son.

One relative recently even wrote to Mr. Sands to have his son declared legally dead.

In the last few months, however, Mr. Sands became deeply interested in the practice of the Presence of God, and he affirmed: "My son is in the Presence of God, and God reveals to me where he is. I know that God brings both of us together in Divine order, and I give thanks." This was his daily prayer.

Shortly thereafter, Mr. Sands introduced me to his son, who had walked into his father's home following an absence of seven long years!

At about the time his father had begun to pray for his son's return, the young man started to look at the telephone directories for his father's name in all the large cities that he visited; he was a traveling salesman. When he arrived in Los Angeles, he discovered his father's name and forthwith took a taxi home. There was great rejoicing!

The Bible says: *"For this my son was dead, and is alive again; he was lost, and is found. And they began to be merry."* (Luke 15:24)

Her Home Was Saved

A few years ago a woman phoned me frantically, saying that a great fire was raging around her property. I told her to join with me over the phone in practicing the Presence of God. We prayed as follows: "We now acknowledge the Presence of God where you and your home are. Your home is surrounded with an envelope of God's love. The whole armor of God surrounds you and your home. You are immersed in the Omnipresence of God. The Presence of God is the cause of peace, harmony, joy, faith, and confidence. The sacred circle of God's eternal love surrounds your home and enfolds it, and God's Overshadowing Presence watches over it. We are now releasing this prayer, knowing that God answers."

The next morning the woman phoned me and said that the fire had burned right up to her back fence and had stopped! It seemed miraculous. Later that morning a policeman visited her, and he exclaimed, "The only thing that could have saved you was God."

She Acknowledged the Presence

A young private secretary in a large legal office in New York wrote me, saying that two girls in the office were viciously gossiping about her and that they were trying to undermine her position. The gossip apparently was severe and wholly unjustified.

I wrote her and suggested that she acknowledge the Presence of God in the girls, which meant a recognition of a superior wisdom, Divine love, superior power, and Divine harmony, plus also the recognition of these powers and qualities in herself. I wrote the following prayer for her:

> I see the Presence of God in these two girls (mentioning their names). God thinks, speaks, and acts through each one of them. They are loving, kind, and cooperative. Whenever I think of either one of them or meet one of them, I silently affirm, "God's love speaks through you. God is working through you."

This was the only action the young woman took. Within a week's time, this young secretary wrote to me, informing me that the two girls were transferred to another office, but before they left, both of them asked her to dinner and expressed their love and appreciation for her. The practice of the Presence dissolved everything unlike Itself in the minds and hearts of these two gossiping women.

His Audience Loves Him Now

A young minister, who came to me for advice, told me that his parishioners were very cold and also highly critical of his sermons. He said that since he had spent many hours preparing his sermons and had adhered closely to the tenets of their faith, he could not understand their coldness and aloofness. In fact, in over a year, he had not been invited to dinner by any member of the congregation. I suggested the practice of the Presence, and he said, "What's that?"

I replied, "Before you go onto the platform, radiate to the audience love, peace, and good will, and affirm boldly for ten minutes: 'All those who come here this morning are blessed, healed, and inspired. God thinks, speaks, and acts through me. God is healing this audience through me. All who hear the words of truth pronounced by me are instantaneously healed, exalted, and prospered in a wonderful way. I love my audience—they are God's children, and God's glory shines through them.'"

After a few weeks had passed, a miraculous change took place. His parishioners began to compliment him and tell him how they were helped and inspired by his sermons and how their prayers were answered in a wonderful way.

The minister had discovered that the cure for every difficulty and problem is to practice the Presence of God. This Presence is the Divine reality of every man, lying dormant beneath the superimposition of man's false beliefs, opinions, superstitions, and mal-conditioning.

How Brother Lawrence Practiced the Presence

Brother Lawrence of the 17th century was a monk. He was a saintly man, and wholly devoted to God. Possessing a great humility and simplicity, he was in tune with the Infinite. "To do the will of God," he said, "is my whole business."

Brother Lawrence practiced the Presence when washing the dishes or scrubbing the floor. His attitude was that it was all God's work. His awareness of the Presence of God was no less when he was employed in the kitchen than when he was before the altar. The way to God was to Brother Lawrence through the heart and through love. His superiors marvelled at the man who, although he was educated only to the point of reading and writing, could express himself with such beauty and profound wisdom. It was the inner voice of God that prompted all his sayings.

This is how Brother Lawrence practiced the Presence: He said in effect, "I have put myself in Your Presence; it is Your business that I am about, and so everything will be all right."

He said that the only sorrow he could experience would be the loss of the sense of His Presence, but he never feared that, being wholly aware of God's love and absolute goodness.

In his early life, he feared that he would be damned. This torture of his mind persisted for four years; then he said that the whole cause of this negativity was lack of faith in God. Having become aware of that, he was freed, and he thereupon entered into a life of continual joy.

Whether he was cooking, baking, or washing pans in the kitchen, Brother Lawrence schooled himself to pause, if only for a moment, to think of God in the center of his being, to be conscious of God's Presence, and to keep a hidden meeting with

Him. Due to his inner illumination when he enjoyed the raptures of the Spirit, he emerged into a realm of profound peace.

He Healed His Son

I received a letter from a businessman in Chicago who had read in my book, *The Miracle of Mind Dynamics*, the chapter entitled, "How to Be Well and Stay Well All the Time;" it appealed to him immensely. His son, aged eight, had been ill for about a year with a serious case of asthma which caused paroxysmal attacks from time to time, requiring emergency treatment.

This father sat down one night by the bedside of his son and prayed out loud while his son was asleep:

> John, you are God's son. I see the Presence of God in you now. This is the presence of harmony, health, peace, joy, vitality, and wholeness. God breathed into you the breath of life. The Spirit of God made you, and I know the breath of the Almighty gave you life. You inhale the peace of God, and you exhale the love of God. *"Father, I thank thee that thou hast heard me. And I knew that thou hearest me always."* (John 11:41–42)

He prayed for about an hour, reiterating these great truths and knowing that they would sink into the subconscious of his boy. He definitely felt that his prayer was answered by a sense of inner peace, and he had no desire to pray any more.

When the little boy awoke in the morning, he said, "Daddy, I had a dream, and an angel appeared to me and said, 'John, you are healed.'" The boy had completely recovered. His father's conviction of the Presence of God was communicated to his son, and the subconscious of the boy dramatized the conviction in the symbolic form of an angelic figure, which made the boy aware that he was made whole. That is an example of the power of the practice of the Presence of God.

He Walked and Talked

Dr. Elsie L. McCoy of Beverly Hills, California, gave me permission to cite the following miraculous healing:

> Mr. A. sustained severe head, neck, and chest injuries when a four hundred pound table had fallen on him. He was unconscious for several days. I called a minister to pray with me, and for about an hour we affirmed together, "God is the life of this man. He is alive with the life of God. The Presence of God in him is the presence of peace, vitality, and wholeness."
>
> At the end of that hour, he regained consciousness, but he was unable to speak or walk because he was paralyzed. It seemed like a hopeless case. I applied everything that I know in the healing arts, but I knew in my heart that only God could heal this man. The minister and I prayed with him, every day, affirming, "God walks and talks in you. You are speaking through the power of God, and you walk freely and joyously. We hear you talking to us, and we see you walking across the room. God is healing you now."
>
> At the end of three months, the miracle happened. He began to speak clearly, and he walked without crutches; he is still walking. His own statement was that he had heard everything that we said and drank it in. Undoubtedly, our prayers entered his subconscious mind, which responded. This was the result of the practice of the power of God to heal.

He Could Not Be Ruined

While writing this chapter, I was interrupted by a long distance telephone call from an old friend. His voice was strident and angry as he said, "My enemies are out to ruin and undermine me and my business." I suggested that he practice the Presence of God as follows:

> These two men (his so-called enemies) are reflecting more and more of God and His goodness every day. They have the same hopes, desires, and aspirations as I have. They desire peace, harmony, love, joy, and abundance, and so do I. They are honest, sincere, and full of integrity, and Divine justice reigns supreme. I wish for them all of God's blessings. Our relationship is harmonious, peaceful, and full of Divine understanding. They wish to do the right thing according to the Golden Rule, as I do. I salute the Divinity within them, and I give thanks for the harmonious solution.

I told him to use this prayer many times a day and to let the impressions and feelings of these thoughts sink into his deeper mind until he was possessed by their truth. Furthermore, I related to him that as he continued to bless in the above way, there would be a great sense of inner release, like a cleansing of the soul. I let him know that he would feel at peace and be relaxed.

He practiced the above technique in a whole-souled, devoted manner, and he discovered that he actually secreted the healing power from the depths of himself which brought about a perfect, harmonious solution in the realm of his relationship to the men in question. A magnificent change took place between them. He discovered the practice of the Presence to be the all-encompassing truth which sets man free.

Practice the Three Steps

The First Step: Accept the fact that God is the only Presence and the only power; God is the very life and reality of you.

The Second Step: Realize, know, and claim that everything you are and everything you see, whether it is a tree, dog, or cat, is a part of God's expression; this is the greatest thing you can do; it is powerful beyond words.

The Third Step: Sit down quietly two or three times a day, and think along these lines: "God is all there is; He is all in all."

Begin to realize that God indwells you and everyone around you. Remind yourself frequently that God is working and thinking through you, and other people as well, and especially remind yourself of this truth when dealing with or doing business with people.

If you sing, speak, act, or play an instrument in public, affirm silently, "God is blessing, prospering, and inspiring the audience through me." This will make them love and appreciate you. This is the real practice of the Presence of God.

Dwelling with God

I live in a state of consciousness. It is the consciousness of inner peace, joy, harmony, and good will for all men. I know that my real country is not a geographical location; a country is a dwelling place. I dwell in the Secret Place of the Most High; I abide in the Shadow of the Almighty; I walk and talk with God all the days of my life. I know that there is only one Divine Family, and that is humanity. *"Let God arise, and his enemies be scattered."* (Psalm 68:1)

I know that my only enemies are fear, ignorance, superstition, compromise, and other false gods. I will not permit these enemies to dwell in my mind. I refuse to give negative thoughts a passport to my mind. I enthrone God and His love in my mind. I think, feel, and act from the standpoint of Divine love. I mentally touch the Divine power now, and It moves in my behalf; I feel invincible.

Peace begins with me. I feel God's river of peace flowing through me now.

I claim that the love of God permeates the hearts of all men, and God and His wisdom rule, guide, and govern me and all men everywhere. God inspires me, our leaders, and the governments of all nations to do His will, and His will only. The will of God is harmony, peace, joy, wholeness, beauty, and perfection. It is wonderful!

RECALLING GREAT TRUTHS

1. The practice of the Presence is the key to health, happiness, and peace of mind.
2. Begin to realize that everything you see is some part of the self-expression of God.
3. God is Infinite Intelligence, and if your son is lost It knows where he is and will reveal to you his whereabouts.
4. Nothing can touch you or your home if you surround yourself with a circle of God's love and know that His Overshadowing Presence protects you.
5. See the Presence of God in the other who is troublesome or who is gossiping about you. Claim that God thinks, speaks, and acts through that person, and you will discover that love never fails.
6. If you are a speaker or lecturer, affirm, "God is blessing and healing the audience through me," and wonders will happen in your life.
7. All work is. God's work, and whatever work you are engaged in, do it for the glory of God.
8. You can pray for a member of your family by realizing the presence of God's love, peace, joy, and harmony. Feel the reality of what you affirm, and the subconscious of your loved one will respond accordingly.
9. If people are trying to hurt you, realize that you are one with God, and they cannot penetrate your defense. Bless them by realizing that they are honest,

sincere, loving, and that they are governed by God and by God alone. There will be a harmonious solution inevitably.

10. Realize that everything you see, regardless of what it is, is part of God's expression; this is the greatest thing you can do. Every man you meet is an incarnation of God. He is waiting for you to overlook his frailties, short-comings, and derelictions, and, like Paul of Tarsus, you should try to see the Christ in him, the hope of glory.